BILL & SUE TELL

WELL-VERSED KIDS

PARENT-TEACHER MANUAL

NAVPRESS

A MINISTRY OF THE NAVIGATORS

The Navigators is an international Christian organization. Jesus Christ gave His followers the Great Commission to go and make disciples (Matthew 28:19). The aim of The Navigators is to help fulfill that commission by multiplying laborers for Christ in every nation.

NavPress is the publishing ministry of The Navigators. NavPress publications are tools to help Christians grow. Although publications alone cannot make disciples or change lives, they can help believers learn biblical discipleship, and apply what they learn to their lives and ministries.

Second Printing, 1988

Printed in the United States of America

CONTENTS

AUTHORS

Bill and Sue Tell met at Hope College in Holland, Michigan, where they were students. They were both involved in student ministries there, and later at Western Michigan University, University of Kentucky, and University of Illinois.

They have been involved with The Navigators since their college days. Bill now works as a field director for The Navigators.

Bill and Sue have two sons, David and Jeff. They live in Sacramento, California.

ACKNOWLEDGMENTS

Well-Versed Kids began as a group effort. Without the help, encouragement, and creativity of many, many friends, it would not be available to you today.

A big "thank you" goes to our beloved church for originally suggesting we work on the development of a Scripture memory program to be used in the elementary departments. Thanks for providing the opportunity for us to write the program and to experiment with it in our church. We've learned much from our experiences.

A special debt of gratitude is due Mrs. Barb Chevalier, Mrs. Kathy Lorimor, and Mrs. Millie Moser, who worked side by side with us on the initial development and implementation of *Well-Versed Kids* in our church. Personally convinced of the value of Scripture memory, they were tremendous motivators, encouragers, and hard workers as together we outlined the program.

> "May the LORD repay you for what you have done. May you be rightly rewarded by the LORD, the God of Israel, under whose wings you have come to take refuge." (Ruth 2:12)

SECTION ONE

I. THE
WELL-VERSED KIDS
PROGRAM

A. CHILDREN, BIBLE MEMORY, AND
WELL-VERSED KIDS

Would children benefit from memorizing the Bible, or is Bible memory one of those old Sunday school ideas that just never seem to die? The answer to both questions is an emphatic "Yes!" Not only do children greatly benefit by memorizing Scripture; Bible memory is God's idea, and as such, will never die. In Colossians 3:16, the Apostle Paul encourages us to "let the word of Christ dwell in you richly."

Elementary children are at the perfect age to begin memorizing God's Word. Children have a tender conscience and are responsive to the truths of God's Word.

Memory work is easy for elementary children. Their sharp, alert minds are hungry to be filled. The elementary years have rightly been called "the Golden Age of Memory."

As children mature into preadolescents, they are defining their moral and spiritual values. These decisions will govern many of their choices during the turbulent teen years. It is imperative that the Holy Spirit has the tool of the Word of God planted in their minds to guide them as they face life's decisions.

Well-Versed Kids builds on these positive qualities God has instilled in children. This Scripture memory program will help you as a parent to "train a child in the way he should go" (Proverbs 22:6).

Well-Versed Kids will heighten your child's awareness of God. By having the Scriptures firmly planted in his or her mind, the Holy Spirit has the means by which to help your child make godly choices.

Well-Versed Kids will help establish the Bible as the ultimate authority in your child's life. You can use whatever version of the Bible you prefer with the *Well-Versed Kids* program.

Well-Versed Kids will give you a structure with which to organize your child's spiritual growth. The basic doctrinal and practical topics, along with the memory verses presented, offer a balanced approach to the Christian life.

Well-Versed Kids will stimulate many rich family times and discussions around the Word of God.

Well-Versed Kids also clearly presents the plan of salvation.

Well-Versed Kids will teach your child the essential aspects of Christian growth and will provide practical helps for developing his or her relationship with God. Your child will become convinced that God is on his side, and will learn to value his relationship with God. A well-versed kid will come to understand that growing as a Christian means positive change.

Well-Versed Kids is more than a Bible memory program. It is a course on Christian living specifically designed for elementary children. Completing *Well-Versed Kids* helps assure that you are laying a spiritual foundation of gold, silver, and costly stones in the life of your child (see 1 Corinthians 3:12).

B. AN OVERVIEW

Your *Well-Versed Kids* package contains:

    108 verse cards
    1 verse pack
    1 verse box
    1 parent-teacher manual

The memory program is divided into six main topics with eighteen verse cards for each topic. The names of the six main topics are at the top of the charts on pages 14-16. The topic names also appear in vertical bars along the edge of each page covering that topic.

Each of the six main topics is divided into subtopics. The main topics and subtopics have been carefully chosen to reflect the needs of elementary children. The beginning subtopics will be easily understood by the youngest student. These subtopics then become progressively more difficult as you advance through the program, with the concluding subtopics designed for the preadolescent. The following chart gives an overview of the entire program.

13

	I. UNDERSTANDING SALVATION	II. KNOWING GOD

LEVEL 1	A1. What is sin? 1 John 5:17
	A2. What is the result of sin? Romans 6:23
	A3. Who saves me from my sin? John 1:29
	A4. What must I do to become a Christian? John 3:16
	A5. Is there any other way? Romans 3:23
	A6. How can I be sure I am a Christian? John 3:36
		A. Jesus the Son
		  1. Luke 1:35
		  2. Matthew 16:16
		  3. Hebrews 13:8
		
		B. Jesus my Savior
		  1. Luke 2:11
		  2. Matthew 1:21
		  3. 1 Timothy 1:15

LEVEL 2	B1. What is sin? James 4:17
	B2. What is the result of sin? John 8:24
	B3. Who saves me from my sin? Romans 5:8
	B4. What must I do to become a Christian? John 5:24
	B5. Is there any other way? Ephesians 2:8-9
	B6. How can I be sure I am a Christian? 1 John 5:13
		C. God the Father
		  1. John 20:17
		  2. Galatians 3:26
		  3. Luke 1:37
		
		D. God, My Creator
		  1. Genesis 1:27
		  2. Psalm 100:3
		  3. Psalm 95:6

LEVEL 3	C1. What is sin? Isaiah 53:6
	C2. What is the result of sin? Isaiah 59:2
	C3. Who saves me from my sin? 1 Peter 3:18
	C4. What must I do to become a Christian? John 1:12
	C5. Is there any other way? John 14:6
	C6. How can I be sure I am a Christian? 1 John 5:11-12
		E. God the Holy Spirit
		  1. 2 Corinthians 13:14
		  2. John 14:26
		  3. 1 Corinthians 2:12
		
		F. The Spirit in Me
		  1. 1 Corinthians 3:16
		  2. Romans 8:9
		  3. Galatians 5:22-23

	III. GROWING AS A CHRISTIAN	IV. ENJOYING GOD

LEVEL 1	A. Listening to God
	  1. Matthew 4:4
	  2. Psalm 119:105
	  3. Psalm 119:11
	
	B. Talking to God
	  1. John 16:24
	  2. 1 John 5:14
	  3. 1 Thessalonians 5:16-18
		A. God Loves Me.
		  1. 1 John 3:16
		  2. Jeremiah 31:3
		  3. 1 John 4:11
		
		B. God Cares About Me.
		  1. 1 Peter 5:7
		  2. Nahum 1:7
		  3. Philippians 4:19

LEVEL 2	C. Obeying God
	  1. James 1:22
	  2. John 14:15
	  3. Psalm 119:44
	
	D. Telling Others
	  1. Acts 1:8
	  2. Mark 5:19
	  3. Mark 16:15
		C. God Gives Me Peace.
		  1. John 14:27
		  2. Philippians 4:7
		  3. 2 Thessalonians 3:16
		
		D. God Protects Me.
		  1. Psalm 91:11
		  2. Psalm 91:14
		  3. Psalm 121:7

LEVEL 3	E. Building Christian Friendships
	  1. Hebrews 10:24
	  2. Hebrews 3:13
	  3. Proverbs 17:17
	
	F. Having Devotions
	  1. Mark 1:35
	  2. Psalm 5:3
	  3. Exodus 33:11
		E. God Helps Me.
		  1. Psalm 121:1-2
		  2. Isaiah 41:10
		  3. Philippians 4:13
		
		F. God Accepts Me.
		  1. Psalm 139:13
		  2. Psalm 139:14
		  3. Psalm 139:15-16

	V. BUILDING CHARACTER	VI. GREAT BIBLE TRUTHS

LEVEL 1	A. Be Obedient to Parents.
	  1. Ephesians 6:1
	  2. Colossians 3:20
	  3. Proverbs 1:8
	
	B. Be Honest.
	  1. Leviticus 19:11
	  2. Colossians 3:9
	  3. Acts 24:16
		A. Forgiveness
		  1. 1 John 1:9
		  2. Colossians 3:13
		  3. Matthew 18:21-22
		
		B. The Bible
		  1. 2 Timothy 3:16
		  2. Mark 13:31
		  3. Proverbs 30:5

LEVEL 2	C. Be Dependable.
	  1. Numbers 23:19
	  2. Luke 16:10
	  3. Proverbs 28:20
	
	D. Be a Servant.
	  1. Mark 10:45
	  2. Ephesians 6:7
	  3. Matthew 20:26
		C. The Second Coming
		  1. Acts 1:11
		  2. Matthew 24:44
		  3. Colossians 3:4
		
		D. The Church
		  1. Ephesians 2:22
		  2. Psalm 122:1
		  3. Ephesians 4:16

LEVEL 3	E. Be Loving.
	  1. 1 Corinthians 13:4
	  2. 1 Corinthians 13:5
	  3. 1 Corinthians 13:6-7
	
	F. Be Committed.
	  1. Romans 12:1
	  2. Romans 12:2
	  3. Romans 12:3
		E. The Lord Is My Shepherd.
		  1. Psalm 23:1
		  2. Psalm 23:2
		  3. Psalm 23:3
		  4. Psalm 23:4
		  5. Psalm 23:5
		  6. Psalm 23:6

C. THE VERSE CARDS

Each verse card has the *New International Version* (NIV) on one side and the *New King James Version* (NKJV) on the other side. To make the cards easy to read and organize, they are large and come in six colors, one color representing each main topic:

Understanding Salvation—gold
Knowing God—blue
Growing as a Christian—peach
Enjoying God—green
Building Character—purple
Great Bible Truths—yellow

The diagram on the following page is an example of an actual verse card.

Every verse has a name (the subtopic) and an address (the reference). A six-year-old child understands the words *name* and *address* better than *topic* and *reference*. The name of the verse is a helpful memory aid. It gives a hint about the meaning of the verse. In memorizing a verse, the name and address should be learned first before learning the actual words of the verse. Throughout the parent-teacher manual, the words *name* and *address* will replace the words *subtopic* and *reference*.

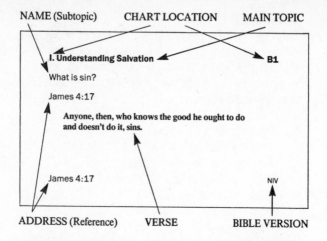

NAME (Subtopic)   CHART LOCATION   MAIN TOPIC

I. Understanding Salvation   **B1**

What is sin?

James 4:17

**Anyone, then, who knows the good he ought to do
and doesn't do it, sins.**

James 4:17   NIV

ADDRESS (Reference)   VERSE   BIBLE VERSION

Memorizing the main topic is optional. The position in
the chart, for example "A1," should *not* be memorized.
These additional letters and numbers would be confusing
to a child. A verse will be considered correctly memorized when the child quotes:

    1. the name (subtopic) of the verse;
    2. the address (reference) of the verse;
    3. the verse with no more than one error;
    4. the address again.

    There are three horizontal levels of verses from top to
bottom in the overview chart. We suggest a child memorize level 1, then level 2, and finally level 3. *This is the
pattern of increasing difficulty.* The major goal of *Well-*

18

Versed Kids is that the student will be able to quote in one sitting the thirty-six verses in each level.

D. THE VERSE PACK

The vinyl, fold-over verse pack with a plastic window is designed to be carried by your child. If he or she has idle minutes, this handy pack will allow your child to redeem the time.

The verse currently being learned should be put in the window. The remaining verses of the main topic being worked on should be kept inside the pack. For example, if a child is memorizing Hebrews 13:8 (from level 1 of "Knowing God"), the other five level-1 verses of "Knowing God" should also be in the pack. Since the first group of "Understanding Salvation" verses has already been learned, these cards may be carried in the pack as well, so that they will be available for review. The pack is capable of holding an entire level, or thirty-six cards, at a time.

E. THE VERSE BOX

The verse box is the permanent home for all 108 *Well-Versed Kids* memory cards. We suggest that the verse box be stored in a special place where it is readily available to you and your child.

F. THE PARENT-TEACHER MANUAL

This manual is essential to the success of your child and *Well-Versed Kids*. It is not an instruction book to be read only once. Rather, it is a verse-by-verse guide to help you lead your child through *Well-Versed Kids*. For each verse in the program, there is an expanded concept statement explaining the key thought of the verse as well as ideas and helps for teaching the verse. The manual also includes answers to some questions your child may ask about the verse.

There are numerous review tips, suggestions for child-sized applications, recommended rewards, and ideas to keep *Well-Versed Kids* a fun project. Some of the memory tips apply only to specific verses. However, many tips are generic and can be used with any verse.

To simplify the content, the manual has been written using words and phrases that refer to one parent working with one child at home. However, *Well-Versed Kids* was first developed for use in Sunday school, and also works well in Christian schools.

II. USING
WELL-VERSED KIDS
IN THE HOME

Parents know their children's capabilities and needs better than anyone. *The memory pace is less important than finishing* Well-Versed Kids *with a positive attitude toward Bible memory*. There are two suggested options for you to choose between as you begin *Well-Versed Kids*.

Option one is a three-year program, covering thirty-six verses in one level per year. The goal here would be to quote all the verses in that level at the end of the year. This option follows the school calendar with memory work, beginning with the start of school and ending with the start of summer vacation. Summers are used for catch-up and review. New verses are learned at the rate of one per week. At the end of every six verses, one week may be taken for review.

Option two is a two-year program. There are 108 verses in *Well-Versed Kids*. If your child memorizes one verse card per week, the program can be completed in just over two years. The goal of the program is the same as in option one: to be able to quote all thirty-six verses in each level at one sitting.

Regardless of the option you choose, the key to success is regularity and consistency. Having a regularly scheduled time to learn and review verses is critical. Using the time while eating breakfast together or driving the children to school can work well for consistent memory work.

III. USING
WELL-VERSED KIDS
IN THE CHURCH

The *Well-Versed Kids* memory program will complement any Sunday school curriculum your church is
currently using. It can also serve as a stand-alone curriculum. By embellishing it with well-chosen Bible stories
and real life applications, a well-balanced picture of the
Christian life is presented to the children by the end of the
program.

Through Scripture memory and review, extended
learning is guaranteed. Studies show that by Wednesday,
children have forgotten seventy percent of what they
learned in Sunday school, even though they were
actively involved in the lesson. However, when an organ-
ized, progressive memory program is a continuing part of
the curriculum, retention is one-hundred percent. The
Word of God permanently planted in the minds of
children has life-changing potential!

Each topic of the *Well-Versed Kids* program is
divided into three levels. The concepts in these three
levels build on each other and become progressively
more difficult. *Well-Versed Kids* can be used for any

three years of an elementary program or it can be expanded to fill all six years. When expanding the program, the second graders review the verses they memorized in first grade, the fourth graders review the verses they memorized in third grade, and the sixth graders review the verses they learned in fifth grade. This works well if the memory program is used with other curriculum materials.

Expanding the program to six years allows an emphasis on review, which is often the missing ingredient in a Bible memory program. This also makes the second year much easier and allows slower children to catch up. Being confident in Scripture memory is a tremendous encouragement to children.

Fitting *Well-Versed Kids* into the yearly calendar is easy. Over the course of one school year or one calendar year, depending on which option is chosen, the elementary children will memorize thirty-six key portions of Scripture. The goal of the program is to have each child accurately quote all thirty-six verses in one sitting. The chart on the following page pictures one of the options for incorporating *Well-Versed Kids* into your church's Sunday school program.

Option one incorporates new memory work into the fall, winter, and spring quarters. Memorize one verse per Sunday for the first twelve Sundays of each quarter. This will leave one Sunday for review and catch-up. The summer quarter, when attendance is often irregular, is used for review and catch up. With this option, *Well-Versed Kids* can be either a three-year or six-year program as just described.

FALL QUARTER	
Understanding Salvation	Knowing God

WINTER QUARTER	
Growing as a Christian	Enjoying God

SPRING QUARTER	
Building Character	Great Bible Truths

Option two enables a child to do new memory work throughout the entire calendar year. A child will have two full months to learn the six verses in each main topic at any level. Learning a new verse at the rate of one per week will leave two or three Sundays before beginning the next topic. These extra Sundays allow time to emphasize application, review, and catch up. As with option one, this option can be used as a three-year or six-year program.

Appendix II gives additional helps for introducing and implementing *Well-Versed Kids* into a Sunday school program.

IV. USING
WELL-VERSED KIDS
IN THE CHRISTIAN
SCHOOL

As in the church, *Well-Versed Kids* can complement the regular Bible curriculum in the Christian school. Because of its balance of doctrine and practical Christian living, it can also be used as the Bible curriculum. At the rate of one verse card per week, the thirty-six verses of each year fit the school calendar perfectly.

Well-Versed Kids is conceptually appropriate for any three grades between grades one and six. You can use this Scripture memory program for all six elementary grades by memorizing levels A and B in first grade, then reviewing in second grade; memorizing levels C and D in third grade and reviewing in fourth; memorizing levels E and F in fifth grade and reviewing in sixth.

Alternating review years with years for learning new verses is highly recommended. Scripture review and long-term retention are often neglected parts of Bible memory. Allowing for review years reinforces the importance of retaining God's Word and increases the likelihood that these verses will be incorporated into the child's memory for a lifetime. With Scripture memory, quality is more important than quantity.

Remembering the memorized verses will be much easier for the children during the review years. With all the challenges and pressures that today's young people face, a year of review can impart a sense of victory, accomplishment, and even enjoyment.

Appendix III lists several additional activities and games that will enhance Bible memory in the classroom.

SECTION TWO

I. UNDERSTANDING SALVATION

The terms *born again* and *saved* are commonly heard in the Christian community. Both communicate that a person is a Christian. A Christian has admitted his sinfulness, has recognized that Jesus paid the penalty for his sin by dying on the cross, and has asked Jesus to come into his life.

What brings a person to this point of decision? For children, it is often a parent's encouragement or a special children's ministry. But few children could explain the gospel message to which they have responded.

The verses in "Understanding Salvation" will help your child clearly understand the gospel message and how to become a Christian.

This first topic in *Well-Versed Kids* is unique in that all the subtopics are in the form of questions that are then answered by the memory verses. (The question is the "name" of the verse.) These questions and answers lead your child through the plan of salvation. In each of the three levels of verses, the questions are the same. However, the verses progressively give more information from one level to the next. You will want to read through all the A, B, and C verses to gain a perspective of what lies ahead.

YOUR MEMORY PLAN

By now you should have selected one of the two options in section one regarding the memory pace. Regardless of the option you choose, your child or children should memorize the entire level (the six main topics with six verses each) before moving to the next level.

MEMORIZING A NEW VERSE

Day 1: Talk about the verse and its meaning with your child. Look up the verse in your child's Bible and let the child underline it. Memorize the name and address of the verse.

Day 2: Check if your child remembers the name, the meaning, and the address of the verse. Memorize the first phrase. That first phrase is vitally important to learning the entire verse.

Day 3: Review the name, address, and first phrase. Memorize the rest of the verse one phrase at a time. Spending time on it at breakfast, dinner, and bedtime will help implant it in your child's mind. Throughout the manual, as well as in Appendix IV, you will find specific ways to help your child memorize.

Days 4-7: Review the name, address, and words of the verse at least once per day.

TOPIC: *I. Understanding Salvation*
SUBTOPIC: *A1. What is sin?*
VERSE: *1 John 5:17*
   All wrongdoing is sin.

CONCEPT

Children understand that there are certain things they are
not to do because to do them would not be right. When
they have decided to do these things, they likely experienced someone's displeasure and discipline. Memorizing
1 John 5:17 now adds a new dimension to wrongdoing:
It is also sin.

COMMUNICATING THE CONCEPT

Any perfect kids here? An essential element for
responding to the gospel is a sense of need that makes us
want what Jesus offers. If we don't have a problem, we
don't need a solution. It's important to communicate that
everyone does wrong and therefore sins. You may want
to ask your child some of the things he or she remembers
doing that were wrong. This keeps children from seeing
themselves as exceptions to this verse.

A growing concept. Children begin to understand
early that there is right and wrong. They also know that
for some reason they don't always do what is right. They
have experienced that their right or wrong behavior
affects others (Dad gets angry!) and themselves (I get
punished!). In this verse we are learning that another
person is affected by our wrongdoing, and that's God.
This is why "all wrongdoing is sin."

Memory tip. Our first *Well-Versed Kids* verse is only four words long. Even though this is an easy start, it is important to start right. Before actually beginning to learn the words of the verse itself, remember to (1) teach the meaning, and (2) memorize the verse's name ("What is sin?") and address (1 John 5:17).

TOPIC: *I. Understanding Salvation*
SUBTOPIC: *A2. What is the result of sin?*
VERSE: *Romans 6:23*
The wages of sin is death.

CONCEPT

All wrongdoing, or sin, needs to be punished. There is not only an immediate punishment from someone like Mom or Dad; there is also a final punishment from God.

COMMUNICATING THE CONCEPT

"Wages." Wages may be a new word. Adults know that wages are earned (they are not a free gift) in exchange for doing something, but children may not. Use a number of illustrations that depict different types of wages given in exchange for varying kinds of "work."

"Wages of sin." Draw some parallels to help the child understand this concept. For example, what you will receive (wages) for washing the car is one dollar. What you will receive (wages) for sinning is death. The child must understand that for every behavior there is a consequence.

"Death." What is meant by death is not easy to communicate correctly. The death that we earn as "the wages of sin" is more than just a physical, bodily death. Man has more than just a physical nature; he also has a spiritual nature. The penalty for sin includes both physical and spiritual death. To be spiritually dead is to experience separation from God, whether we are physically alive or dead. After we die physically, those who are spiritually dead "will go away to eternal punishment" (Matthew 25:46).

The big picture. Now may be a good time to go through and summarize the remainder of part A in "Understanding Salvation" to help give the big picture and impart some hope!

TOPIC: *I. Understanding Salvation*
SUBTOPIC: *A3. Who saves me from my sin?*
VERSE: *John 1:29*
"Look, the Lamb of God, who takes away the sin of the world!"

CONCEPT

In our first two memory verses, we discovered that we have two problems: first, we have sinned; and second, we will receive the consequences of that sin. Just as there are two problems, there are two solutions. The first is stated in John 1:29—Jesus came to take away sin.

COMMUNICATING THE CONCEPT

"Look, the Lamb of God." John the Baptist is introducing Jesus and calls Him, "The Lamb of God." The people hearing this may have thought of two things. First, they may have thought of their ancestors who lived in Egypt with Moses during the ten plagues (Exodus 7-12). The last plague was that the oldest child in every Egyptian family would die if Pharaoh did not let God's people leave Egypt. God told Moses that if the Jews would kill a perfect lamb and put some of its blood over their front doors, when He punished the Egyptians, He would pass by their houses and not punish them with death. The blood of the lamb would save them. John the Baptist said that Jesus was like that lamb. His death will protect us from the penalty of sin, spiritual death.

The second thing they probably thought of was the lambs they sacrificed daily in the Temple as a substitute penalty for their sin. Sin must be punished by death and Jesus has taken our place and punishment for us.

"Takes away." This phrase doesn't mean that Jesus totally eliminates sin from our lives. Even the Apostle Paul said, "I really want to do right, but I can't. I do what I don't want to" (Romans 7:15, TLB). Jesus does eliminate and take away the wages of sin, so in that sense, it's as if sin is gone.

How did He do this? He did this by loving us so much that He accepted our penalty and died in our place.

TOPIC: *I. Understanding Salvation*
SUBTOPIC: *A4. What must I do to become a Christian?*
VERSE: *John 3:16*
"For God so loved the world that he gave his one and only Son, that whoever believes in him shall not perish but have eternal life."

CONCEPT

In John 1:29 we saw the facts of the solution: Jesus came to take away sin. The second part of the solution is our response to these facts.

COMMUNICATING THE CONCEPT

What's a Christian? A Christian is a believer in and a follower of Jesus Christ. A Christian has the guilt and punishment of his sins taken away. Instead of having the punishment of death, he or she has received the gift of eternal life.

"The world." *World* refers to people, not rocks, mountains, etc. God loves every person in the world, no matter where he lives, the color of his skin, or the language he speaks.

Watch out for assumptions. Children will faithfully memorize Scripture without ever understanding the meaning and without ever letting you know that they have no idea what it means! Be very careful not to assume that what is obvious to you is understood by your child.

Assumption alert! Did you assume your child knew that "one and only Son" refers to Jesus?

"Believes." We accept it as a fact, with confidence and trust, that Jesus died to save us from our sin and to give us eternal life. If we truly believe something, we will act as though it is true.

"Perish." To perish is to receive the wages of sin and experience physical and spiritual death.

"Eternal." Our life will go on forever—for a while here on earth, and then for the rest of time in Heaven with God.

Personalize it. After John 3:16 is memorized correctly, ask your child to quote it to you, inserting his or her name in place of "the world" and "whoever."

TOPIC: *I. Understanding Salvation*
SUBTOPIC: *A5. Is there any other way to become a Christian?*
VERSE: *Romans 3:23*
All have sinned and fall short of the glory of God.

CONCEPT

"Can't I avoid the wages of sin and still get eternal life just by not sinning?" Not sinning could be another way to God if it was possible, but God's Word says that every person has sinned.

COMMUNICATING THE CONCEPT

Review. Take this opportunity for your child to review 1 John 5:17 and the meaning of sin.

"Fall short of the glory of God." God's ideal for us is to be like Him—that would be wonderful and glorious. However, when we sin, we "fall short" of the ideal. When God looks at us, He sees us as less than perfect. "Yes, all have sinned; all fall short of God's glorious ideal" (Romans 3:23, TLB).

Everybody? Inquire about some people that your child highly respects, and ask if even they sin.

Memory help. Visual aids always enhance learning. Tell how the early copies of the Bible were written on scrolls. Then help your "well-versed kid" make a scroll containing this verse or other verses that he or she may be having difficulty learning. As the child unrolls the scroll, have him or her read the verse out loud. Reading, writing, and speaking all enhance memorization.

TOPIC: *I. Understanding Salvation*
SUBTOPIC: *A6. How can I be sure I am a Christian?*
VERSE: *John 3:36*
"Whoever believes in the Son has eternal life."

CONCEPT

The Bible tells us that believing in Jesus is the only requirement for eternal life. If we believe in Christ we can be assured of our salvation. God does not lie (Numbers 23:19).

COMMUNICATING THE CONCEPT

Review. Before memorizing John 3:36, ask again the questions printed on the previous five cards. Ask for the answers in your child's own words. When you are sure he or she understands, proceed to memorize this verse.

"I don't feel like a Christian today." A number of things may affect how children feel. They may have just "blown it" and not feel like they are good enough to be a Christian. Perhaps they just don't feel well. Whatever the case, we need to understand that our salvation does not depend on how we feel, but on the fact that Jesus died for us and that we believe it. Our salvation is based on fact, not on feeling.

TOPIC: *I. Understanding Salvation*
SUBTOPIC: *B1. What is sin?*
VERSE: *James 4:17*
Anyone, then, who knows the good he ought to do and doesn't do it, sins.

CONCEPT

In 1 John 5:17, we defined sin as doing wrong. Here we see that sin is also not doing what we know is right and good.

COMMUNICATING THE CONCEPT

Knowing is not enough! This concept comes up many times in the Scriptures. Knowing what is right doesn't count unless we do it. If we know it is right to do our chores, but we don't, because we don't feel like it, this is sin. If we know we should be patient but we get angry anyway, then we sin. If we know we should pray and read the Bible, and we don't do it, then that is sin. There are two ways we can sin: by doing wrong (which memory verse teaches this?) or by not doing right.

TOPIC: *I. Understanding Salvation*
SUBTOPIC: *B2. What is the result of sin?*
VERSE: *John 8:24*
"I told you that you would die in your sins; if you do not believe that I am the one I claim to be, you will indeed die in your sins."

CONCEPT

Apart from faith in Jesus Christ, the result of our sins will be death. Sin and death are partners; they go together.

COMMUNICATING THE CONCEPT

Inside out. It is easier to understand John 8:24 if you start in the middle.

"I am." The words *I am* refer to Jesus. He is the one speaking.

"The one I claim to be." Jesus made a lot of claims about Himself, but perhaps one of the most relevant for us here is John 11:25:

> "Jesus said . . . 'I am the resurrection and the life. He who believes in me will live.'"

Jesus claimed that those who believe in Him will not experience the consequences of sin.

Front and back. The beginning and the ending of John 8:24 are the same. Unless we look to Jesus as the solution for our sin problem, we will suffer the result of our sin, which is death.

Devotional help. The Gospel of John contains seven claims that Jesus made about Himself, all in the form of "I am." Discuss one each day in family devotions to help add meaning to John 8:24 (John 6:48, 8:12, 8:58, 10:7, 10:14, 11:25, 14:6).

TOPIC: *I. Understanding Salvation*
SUBTOPIC: *B3. Who saves me from my sin?*
VERSE: *Romans 5:8*

God demonstrates his own love for us in this: While we were still sinners, Christ died for us.

CONCEPT

In the midst of our sinfulness, Jesus willingly paid the penalty for our sin.

COMMUNICATING THE CONCEPT

"I'm not good enough." Sometimes we feel that we are not good enough to become Christians. However, being good enough has nothing to do with it! Romans 5:8 says that God loved us while we were sinners and that Christ died for us while we were sinners.

"Who saves me from my sin?" Not me—I am not saved by being good. Jesus saved me by dying for me.

More than words. God *says* He loves us, but He did more than say it; He *demonstrated* it. How did He do that? How should we respond to that demonstration? Our next memory verse will also give an answer.

I know of no other single practice in the Christian life more rewarding, practically speaking, than memorizing Scripture. . . . No other single discipline is more useful and rewarding than this. No other single exercise pays greater spiritual dividends![1]

TOPIC: *I. Understanding Salvation*
SUBTOPIC: *B4. What must I do to become a Christian?*
VERSE: *John 5:24*

> *"I tell you the truth, whoever hears my word and believes him who sent me has eternal life and will not be condemned; he has crossed over from death to life."*

CONCEPT

How should we respond to God's demonstration of love? (See Romans 5:8.) The above verse tells us of a two-fold response: hearing and believing.

COMMUNICATING THE CONCEPT

"I tell you the truth." Jesus is speaking. In His day, using the phrase *I tell you the truth* was the strongest way of communicating that what He was about to say was very important. Today, we might say something like, "Listen up. This is really important."

Hearing plus believing equals eternal life. *Hear* means to accept the God-given authority of Jesus' words. We believe to be true those things that He said about sin and salvation. To "believe him who sent me" is to accept as true the fact that God sent Jesus to die for our sin.

"Not be condemned." To "condemn" is to declare a sinner guilty and worthy of punishment. Faith in Jesus Christ saves us from the penalty of sin, which is death. "Therefore, there is now no condemnation for those who are in Christ Jesus" (Romans 8:1).

"Crossed over from death to life." This phrase is another way of saying that we are no longer condemned and now have eternal life.

Belief requires action. The story is told of a man who strung a tightrope across Niagara Falls and then walked across the deep gorge on that narrow wire. After he made it all the way across, he asked the crowd, "Who believes I can wheel a wheelbarrow across on the tightrope?" A number of the spectators raised their hands, indicating they believed that the tightrope walker could do it. He then pointed at one of them and said, "Okay, get in the wheelbarrow." The spectator wouldn't do it! Did that spectator really believe that the man could wheel the wheelbarrow across? True belief results in action.

To truly believe that Jesus saves us from sin and gives us eternal life, we need to take action.

1. We need to tell God that we realize we have hurt Him by our sin and that we are sorry.
2. We must tell God that we believe Jesus died for us and invite Jesus to come in and control our lives.
3. Then we need to thank Him for His gift of eternal life.

TOPIC: *I. Understanding Salvation*
SUBTOPIC: *B5. Is there any other way to become a Christian?*
VERSE: *Ephesians 2:8-9*

It is by grace you have been saved, through faith—and this not from yourselves, it is the gift of God—not by works, so that no one can boast.

CONCEPT

Our salvation is not based on anything we can do to earn it. It is a free gift from God to us.

COMMUNICATING THE CONCEPT

"**Grace.**" In Ephesians 2:8, grace is God's love focused on the guilty, undeserving sinner. It is God's grace that treats Christians, even though we are guilty, as though we never sinned. Grace is the opposite of works. Grace is a gift; it is undeserved and unearned love.

"**Through faith—and this not from yourselves.**" The grace is God's part; the faith is our part. Yet even the ability to have faith and believe is a gift from God! No part of salvation can be earned. There is nothing we can do. There is no other way.

"**Not by works.**" The words *not by works* reinforce what has already been said—there is nothing we can do to earn salvation. We can't earn it by going to church, by trying to be good, or by any other way. It is a gift we accept from God.

TOPIC: *I. Understanding Salvation*
SUBTOPIC: *B6. How can I be sure I am a Christian?*
VERSE: *1 John 5:13*
I write these things to you who believe in the name of the Son of God so that you may know that you have eternal life.

CONCEPT
If we believe in Jesus Christ, then we can know for sure that we have eternal life.

COMMUNICATING THE CONCEPT
To whom? To whom is the Apostle John writing? If we are Christians, then this verse applies to us.

What does John want us to understand? Our salvation is based on facts. John wants us to understand that if we believe in Christ, we can know for sure that we have eternal life. *Know* means to know absolutely, without any doubt or question.

The fact of our salvation, when accompanied by the personal experience of a changed and godly life, will lead us to a strong assurance of salvation. Experience does not alter fact; however, it does serve to enhance it.

"Believe in the name." This phrase means that we believe in all that the name Jesus Christ stands for: love, salvation, forgiveness, grace, etc.

TOPIC: *I. Understanding Salvation*
SUBTOPIC: *C1. What is sin?*
VERSE: *Isaiah 53:6*

> *We all, like sheep, have gone astray,*
> *each of us has turned to his own way;*
> *and the LORD has laid on him the iniquity*
> *of us all.*

CONCEPT

Sin here is simply defined as self-centered independence—going our own way and doing our own thing.

COMMUNICATING THE CONCEPT

"We all." Isaiah 53:6 describes everyone. Review Romans 3:23.

"Like sheep." The Bible often compares people to sheep. Sheep are very independent animals that often wander off. We will be looking at the nature of sheep more closely under the topic of "Great Bible Truths" when we learn Psalm 23.

"Gone astray . . . turned to his own way." These words highlight our self-centered independence. We like to do our own thing our own way. We don't like to follow the directions or obey the rules given to us by others, even those given by God. Ignoring God and doing whatever we want is sin.

"The LORD has laid on him." God sent Jesus Christ ("him") to take our sin and to accept our punishment.

"Iniquity." Don't assume the child understands the word *iniquity*. Basically, it is a synonym for *sin*.

TOPIC: *I. Understanding Salvation*
SUBTOPIC: *C2. What is the result of sin?*
VERSE: *Isaiah 59:2*
> *Your iniquities have separated you from your God.*

CONCEPT
Sin always separates. Apart from Christ, the separation is that we are not related to God as our Father (John 1:12).

COMMUNICATING THE CONCEPT
"The Bridge." The Navigators publish a tract called *The Bridge to Life* to illustrate the gospel message. The diagram below is the first part of the illustration. We will add to it as we cover the next few verses.

Sin separates. Sin creates a gulf between each of us and God.

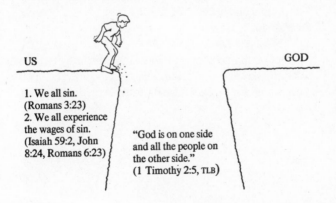

US   GOD

1. We all sin.
(Romans 3:23)
2. We all experience
the wages of sin.
(Isaiah 59:2, John
8:24, Romans 6:23)

"God is on one side
and all the people on
the other side."
(1 Timothy 2:5, TLB)

TOPIC: *I. Understanding Salvation*
SUBTOPIC: *C3. Who saves me from my sin?*
VERSE: *1 Peter 3:18*

> *Christ died for sins once for all, the righteous for the unrighteous, to bring you to God.*

CONCEPT

Christ died for our sins, so that the gulf could be bridged and the separation eliminated.

COMMUNICATING THE CONCEPT

"Once for all." Jesus died once and for all for everyone. His one-time sacrifice is very different from the sacrificial lambs that were sacrificed day after day in the Temple as sin offerings.

"The righteous for the unrighteous." Jesus Christ is the righteous One. He is perfect and lived a life of perfect obedience. We are the unrighteous, because we all sin.

"The Bridge to Life." Jesus is the Bridge over the gulf of sin that separates us from God. Through Jesus we can cross over to God's side, from death to life. This good news is added to the Bridge illustration on the following page.

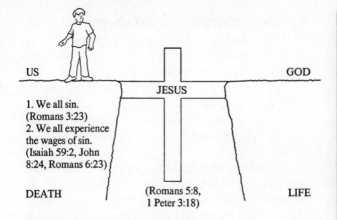

TOPIC: *I. Understanding Salvation*
SUBTOPIC: *C4. What must I do to become a Christian?*
VERSE: *John 1:12*
To all who received him, to those who believed in his name, he gave the right to become children of God.

CONCEPT

By believing and receiving Christ, you can "cross the Bridge" and become a child of God.

COMMUNICATING THE CONCEPT

"Received . . . believed." These two words, *received* and *believed*, help to define each other. To believe in Christ is to receive Christ into your life. It is as if Jesus is knocking at the door of your heart, which is the door of your life, but there is no doorknob on the outside where He is. He will not barge His way into your life. If you want Him to come in, you need to open the door and invite Him in.

Belief requires action. If there is a stream or river near where you live, you may *know* there is a bridge across it. But knowing there is a bridge to use does not mean you are on the other side. To cross to the other side requires action. In the same way, *knowing* that Jesus is the way to God is not enough. You must believe and receive. You can do this by praying a prayer like this: "Lord Jesus, please forgive me for my sin. I am sorry. I believe that You died for me. Please come into my life as my Savior and Lord and give me the gift of eternal life. Thank You for doing this for me."

Completing the picture. Adding this truth—that belief requires action—to the Bridge illustration makes it look like the completed version on the following page.

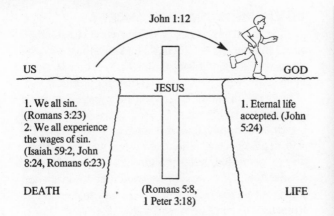

TOPIC: *I. Understanding Salvation*
SUBTOPIC: *C5. Is there any other way to become a Christian?*
VERSE: *John 14:6*
> *Jesus answered, "I am the way and the truth and the life. No one comes to the Father except through me."*

CONCEPT

Jesus knew people would ask, "Is there any other way to God?" The answer He gave was "No!"

COMMUNICATING THE CONCEPT

The context. Jesus is talking with His disciples about Heaven and tells them, "You know the way to the place where I am going" (John 14:4). Thomas didn't understand what Jesus was talking about and asked, "Lord, we don't know where you are going, so how can we know the way?" (verse 5). John 14:6 is Jesus' answer.

One of many? Jesus did not say, "I am *a* way." He said, "I am *the* way." There is only one way to God, one way to eternal life, and that is through belief in Christ.

Review. Now would be a good time to review the previous verses on the subject of the way to eternal life, Romans 3:23 and Ephesians 2:8-9.

TOPIC: *I. Understanding Salvation*
SUBTOPIC: *C6. How can I be sure I am a Christian?*
VERSE: *1 John 5:11-12*
This is the testimony: God has given us eternal life, and this life is in his Son. He who has the Son has life; he who does not have the Son of God does not have life.

CONCEPT

How can I be sure I am a Christian? If I have Jesus in my life, I have eternal life. It's not dependent on anything else.

COMMUNICATING THE CONCEPT

"The testimony." A testimony is a "statement or affirmation of a fact."[2] First John 5:11-12 is God's own testimony about His Son, Jesus.

"God gave us eternal life." These words again remind us that eternal life is an unearned gift. Which previous memory verses say something about this?

"And this life is in his Son." Eternal life and Jesus Christ go together. When does eternal life begin? The Apostle John tells us it begins right now. The verb *has* is in the present perfect tense. This means past action extending to the present. God gave Jesus to pay the penalty for our sins in the past. When we accept Jesus as our Savior, we have eternal life, right now in the present.

NOTES: 1. Charles R. Swindoll, *Growing Strong in the Seasons of Life* (Portland, Oreg.: Multnomah Press, 1983), page 53.

2. *Standard College Dictionary* (New York: Harcourt, Brace & World, 1963), page 1384.

II. KNOWING GOD

Becoming a Christian starts a lifelong process of getting to know God. Knowing God involves understanding that God is three Persons: God the Father, God the Son, and God the Holy Spirit.

In level one of "Knowing God," *Well-Versed Kids* begins with three important truths about Jesus: He is God; He never changes; and He is our Savior. Jesus is very often the most easily understood member of the Trinity. Because He was born and lived on earth, the youngest elementary child will be able to comprehend these truths.

In level two of "Knowing God," God the Father is presented. "Whose Father is God?" "How does He become our Father?" "What is God like?" These are questions that will be answered for the child as the verses are memorized.

God the Holy Spirit is presented last because He is the most difficult to understand. Memorizing these verses will give your children an excellent start in understanding the Spirit of God.

YOUR REVIEW PLAN

The importance of having a regular review plan is highlighted by Garry Friesen in his article, "Painless Scripture Memory": "The only sure dike against verse leakage is regular review."[1] "Review works by the law of *increasing* [emphasis added] returns. The longer you review a verse, the less time you must spend to keep it fresh."[2]

1. Continue memorizing one new verse a week. Use the method explained on page 32.
2. Review daily all the "Understanding Salvation" verses. (This should take about two minutes.)
3. As each "Knowing God" verse is memorized, add it to the "Understanding Salvation" verses to review daily.

When all the "Knowing God" verses have been learned, your child should be able to quote twelve verses, giving each verse's name, address, verse, and address. At this point, depending on the option you choose, you may want to take one or two weeks off from memorizing new verses to concentrate on review and application.

TOPIC: *II. Knowing God*
SUBTOPIC: *A. Jesus the Son*
VERSE: *(1) Luke 1:35*
"The holy one to be born will be called the Son of God."

CONCEPT

God Himself, speaking through an angel, calls Jesus His Son.

COMMUNICATING THE CONCEPT

Who's speaking? Mary, Jesus' mother, is having a discussion with an angel about the coming birth of her child. God often uses angels for servants. This angel was a messenger, and the message was very important: Jesus is the Son of God!

"Holy one." These words show that Jesus would be set apart by God for a special job. Ask your child, "What was Jesus' special job?" John 1:29 from "Understanding Salvation" answers that question.

Who are your parents? All of us have two human parents. Possibly we don't live with them now, or maybe they are no longer alive. However, every person who has ever lived has had a human mother and father except one. Jesus is unique. Mary is Jesus' mother; God is His Father. Therefore, Jesus is called the Son of God.

TOPIC: *II. Knowing God*
SUBTOPIC: *A. Jesus the Son*
VERSE: *(2) Matthew 16:16*
"You are the Christ, the Son of the living God."

CONCEPT

In the previous memory verse (Luke 1:35), God called Jesus His Son. In this memory verse, a person named Simon Peter acknowledges that Jesus is the Son of God.

COMMUNICATING THE CONCEPT

Who's speaking? Simon Peter is speaking. In Matthew 16:13-17, we discover that many people were confused about Jesus' identity. But Peter was not confused. In response to Jesus' own question concerning His identity, Peter quickly replied, "You are the Christ, the Son of the living God."

"You are the Christ." "Christ" is often used as a synonym for "Jesus." They are two *different* names for one Person. The name *Jesus* means "Savior" (Matthew 1:21), the One who shed His blood for sinners. The title *Christ* means "Messiah," or "Anointed King." Jesus was this long-awaited King.

"Living God." God is eternal. He is alive today and always will be. God never changes. What is true about God yesterday is true today and will be true tomorrow.

Parent-teacher help. Peter did not hesitate to answer Jesus' question. He had had daily exposure to Jesus for many months, and therefore his response was instantaneous and sure. A child's faith will develop like Peter's with daily exposure to Jesus. In helping children memorize the verses in *Well-Versed Kids*, continually emphasize the *person* of Jesus, not only verses from the Bible.

TOPIC: *II. Knowing God*
SUBTOPIC: *A. Jesus the Son*
VERSE: *(3) Hebrews 13:8*
Jesus Christ is the same yesterday and today and forever.

CONCEPT
Not only does the "living God" of Matthew 16:16 never change, but Jesus as God's Son never changes.

COMMUNICATING THE CONCEPT
Quiz! An important aspect of Jesus' unchanging nature is His unchanging love for us. To help your child understand this concept, ask these questions:

What are some things you know about Jesus?
How does Jesus feel about you?

One of the answers might be that He loves us. At this point ask questions like:

Will Jesus love you if you knock over your milk?
(make a mistake).
Will Jesus love you if you tell a lie? (commit a sin).
Will Jesus love you if you fail a test? (experience a
disappointment).

The answer to all of these is YES! Jesus never changes.

TOPIC: *II. Knowing God*
SUBTOPIC: *B. Jesus, my Savior*
VERSE: *(1) Luke 2:11*
*"Today in the town of David a Savior has
been born to you; he is Christ the Lord."*

CONCEPT

The concept here is simply that Jesus was born to be *our*
Savior.

COMMUNICATING THE CONCEPT

When? "Today" refers to the day of Jesus' birth. We
celebrate this as Christmas.

Where? The "town of David" is another name for
Bethlehem (Luke 2:4). According to 1 Samuel 16:1,
David's father, Jesse, was from Bethlehem. The Old
Testament prophecy regarding Jesus' birth in Bethlehem
is in Micah 5:2.

Who? "A Savior . . . Christ the Lord." The next

memory verse teaches what Jesus saves us from. This could be a good time to review the verses of "Understanding Salvation."

Memory aid. The answers to the above questions—"when," "where," and "who"—will help your child keep the verse in its correct order.

Is Jesus' actual birthday December 25? We don't know the exact date that Jesus was born. There is no authoritative historical evidence. December 25 started out as the date of a pagan festival when the Romans celebrated the sun. The church of Rome, unable to stamp out this pagan festival, changed it sometime around the year 336 to a celebration of the birth of *the Son*.

TOPIC: *II. Knowing God*
SUBTOPIC: *B. Jesus, my Savior*
VERSE: *(2) Matthew 1:21*
"She will give birth to a son, and you are to give him the name Jesus, because he will save his people from their sins."

CONCEPT

Luke 2:11 taught that Jesus was born to be our Savior. Matthew 1:21 amplifies why we need a Savior: because we need to be saved from our sins!

COMMUNICATING THE CONCEPT

The announcement of the birth. The announcement of Jesus' birth was special in many ways.

1. It was made by an angel.
2. It happened months before His actual birth.
3. It stated that the baby would be a boy.
4. It gave the baby's name.
5. It gave the reason for His name.

Read Luke 2:1-15 with your "well-versed kid" and see how many other ways the announcement of Jesus' birth was unique.

The reason for the birth. Jesus was born to provide a solution to the sin problem. God is holy and He hates sin. He knew that we could not help sinning, so He graciously provided the payment for our sin: Jesus. "He will save his people from their sins."

An analogy. To reinforce the concept that Jesus is the only solution to the sin problem, you might use the analogy of the game of tag. In tag, the person who is "it" is to be avoided, and "home" is safe. Explain that "it" represents sin and that "home" represents safety with Jesus. Only Jesus saves us from our sin. Only at "home" are we safe from "it."

TOPIC: *II. Knowing God*
SUBTOPIC: *B. Jesus, my Savior*
VERSE: *(3) 1 Timothy 1:15*
  Christ Jesus came into the world to save sinners.

CONCEPT

Jesus came into the world with a very specific purpose: that whoever would believe in Him would be saved from his sins.

COMMUNICATING THE CONCEPT

Making it real. Page through an encyclopedia, or perhaps old issues of *National Geographic*, to find pictures of different races of people to help emphasize the concept of the world. At the end, you may want to include a picture of the child to help personalize this verse. Discuss with your child the fact that Jesus came to save all of those people from their sin.

Review.

The title *Christ* means . . . (Matthew 16:16).
The name *Jesus* means . . . (Matthew 1:21).
Why was Jesus born? (Matthew 1:21).
Who will Jesus save from sin? (Matthew 1:21,
    1 Timothy 1:15).

TOPIC: *II. Knowing God*
SUBTOPIC: *C. God the Father*
VERSE: *(1) John 20:17*
"I am returning to my Father and your Father, to my God and your God."

CONCEPT

In this first verse under "God the Father," Jesus clearly and simply states that God is both His Father and our Father.

COMMUNICATING THE CONCEPT

Who is returning? Jesus is returning! He makes the statement in John 20:17 after His resurrection from the dead and is addressing Mary outside the tomb. He is referring to His Ascension, when He would return to Heaven (Acts 1:4-11). It took place forty days later.

"My Father . . . your Father." Jesus was God's Son by birth. We are God's children by adoption.

"My Father . . . my God." It is important to understand that "my Father" and "my God" are synonymous and that "your Father" and "your God" are synonymous. Jesus is identifying God as His Father, and also as our Father, if we have accepted Christ as our Savior. This draws together the concept of "God the Father."

Memory tip. If a verse fits a familiar tune or can be learned to a beat, memory will be enhanced. Try saying John 20:17 rhythmically. You may want to try clapping your hands while you say it. Notice how quickly the child learns the verse.

TOPIC: *II. Knowing God*
SUBTOPIC: *C. God the Father*
VERSE: *(2) Galatians 3:26*
  You are all sons of God through faith in
  Christ Jesus.

CONCEPT

God becomes our Father when we become Christians by
putting our faith in Jesus Christ.

COMMUNICATING THE CONCEPT

  "You . . . all." "You . . . all" are the *Christians* that
Paul is writing to in the province of Galatia. God is not
everyone's Father. Some unbelieving Jews in John 8:41
said to Jesus, "The only Father we have is God himself."
Jesus replied, "If God were your Father, you would love
me. . . . You belong to your father, the devil" (John
8:42,44). God becomes our Father when we ask Jesus to
be our Savior.

TOPIC: *II. Knowing God*
SUBTOPIC: *C. God the Father*
VERSE: *(3) Luke 1:37*
  "Nothing is impossible with God."

CONCEPT

God is able to do whatever He wants to do. What God wants to do is always the best for everyone.

COMMUNICATING THE CONCEPT

Omnipotence. This verse communicates one of God the Father's many attributes, namely His omnipotence, or unlimited power. He can do what He wants. Does this mean God can do anything? No! There are many things that God cannot do. He cannot lie (Numbers 23:19); He cannot tempt people (James 1:13); He cannot destroy change (James 1:17); He cannot be unfaithful (2 Timothy 2:13); and He cannot destroy all life by flooding the earth again (Genesis 9:11-16). He has power to do whatever His will is, and His will is always good, acceptable, and perfect (Romans 12:2).

Two other big words. Two other characteristics of God are fun to introduce at this time. The first is *omniscience*. God knows all things—past, present, and future. Psalm 139:1-7,13-16 is a beautiful summary of God's knowledge as it relates to us as individuals. The second big word is *omnipresence*. God is completely present everywhere. Psalm 139:7-12 makes this big word very personal and comforting.

TOPIC: *II. Knowing God*
SUBTOPIC: *D. God, my Creator*
VERSE: *(1) Genesis 1:27*
God created man in his own image, in the image of God he created him; male and female he created them.

CONCEPT

God created the first man and the first woman.

COMMUNICATING THE CONCEPT

"**In the image of God.**" This phrase is not easy to understand, so let's start with what it does not mean. It does not mean that our body is like God's. The Bible teaches us that "God is spirit" (John 4:24). When the Scriptures say that Adam and Eve were created in the *image* of God, it probably refers to a number of things.

1. Man is different from the animals that God created. They only have a physical nature, but man has both a physical and a spiritual nature. Because of this spiritual nature, we have an eternal nature similar to God's. The issue for us is where we will spend eternity, enjoying God's presence or separated from Him.
2. God is a person, and so are we. We have a personality like God's in that we can think, make decisions, etc. Sin has greatly marred this likeness.
3. God is holy, and the first man was created sinless.

This part of the image was destroyed by sin.

4. God is love, and He made us loving. Sin makes us self-centered and unloving.
5. God is the sovereign Ruler of the universe, and He made man to rule over the earth.

When we come to Christ, this image begins to be restored. We clothe ourselves "with the new [spiritual self], which is (ever in the process of being) renewed *and* remoulded . . . after the image of Him Who created it" (Colossians 3:10, AMP).

TOPIC: *II. Knowing God*
SUBTOPIC: *D. God, my Creator*
VERSE: *(2) Psalm 100:3*
Know that the LORD is God. It is he who made us, and we are his; we are his people, the sheep of his pasture.

CONCEPT
Not only did God create Adam and Eve, the first man and woman, but He also created you and me. Because God created us, we belong to God.

COMMUNICATING THE CONCEPT
An art activity. Give your "well-versed kid" some building blocks, Legos, or perhaps Popsickle sticks and

glue. Ask him or her to make something. When your child finishes, discuss the creation.

Who does your creation belong to?
Why does it belong to you?

Be sure to communicate to your child that just as he created whatever he made and it belongs to him, so God created him and he belongs to God.

A memory aid. Asking questions about a verse helps to fix the verse in your mind. If you have more than one child working on *Well-Versed Kids*, pair them up to ask each other the following questions. If not, you can ask your child the questions yourself. The first time through, your child can look at the verse; the second time, he can recite it from memory.

What is the name of Psalm 100:3?
Is the first word of Psalm 100:3 "yes"?
What is the first word of Psalm 100:3?
What am I supposed to know?
What did God do?
Who do I belong to?
What does God call me?
Where do sheep live?
What is the address of this verse?

TOPIC: *II. Knowing God*
SUBTOPIC: *D. God, my Creator*
VERSE: *(3) Psalm 95:6*
Come, let us bow down in worship, let us kneel before the LORD our maker.

CONCEPT

Because God created you and me and we belong to Him, we should worship Him.

COMMUNICATING THE CONCEPT

Worship. Worship is something we do to honor God. It involves reading and possibly teaching from the Bible. Worship also includes praying to and praising God. It may be done with other people or by yourself.

"Bow down . . . kneel." These are positions of subordination, respect, and worship. The person kneeling is saying by his posture that the one he is kneeling before is more important, is worthy of respect and worship. Shadrach, Meshach, and Abednego, three friends of Daniel, were thrown into the fiery furnace because they would not bow down and worship anyone other than God (Daniel 3). The lordship of Jesus Christ is acknowledged in Philippians 2:10: "At the name of Jesus every knee should bow."

A personal worship service. Have your child write a thank-you letter to God. In it have him or her thank God for all the things he or she has learned about God by memorizing the verses in *Well-Versed Kids.* Then suggest that you and your child get in a kneeling

72

position. In that position, have him or her read or pray the written letter to God. You have just had your own personal worship service.

TOPIC: *II. Knowing God*
SUBTOPIC: *E. God the Holy Spirit*
VERSE: *(1) 2 Corinthians 13:14*
May the grace of the Lord Jesus Christ, and the love of God, and the fellowship of the Holy Spirit be with you all.

CONCEPT
In this first verse on the Holy Spirit, the Spirit is seen as part of the Trinity.

COMMUNICATING THE CONCEPT
The Trinity. With the introduction of this memory verse on the Holy Spirit, we have now introduced all three Persons of God: God the Father, God the Son, and God the Holy Spirit.

The concept of the Trinity is difficult to accurately define. God is one, yet there are three distinct individuals or persons in which God's being exists. All three Persons of the Trinity are divine and eternal, but each has a unique role and relationship to the others.

73

God the Father is the Planner of the work of
redemption, creation, and providence.

God the Son is the Creator of all things (John
1:3,10), the Light that gives light to every man
(John 1:9), and the Redeemer of man by His birth,
death, and resurrection (Ephesians 1:3-14).

God the Holy Spirit dwells in all believers. This
indwelling of the Spirit happens when we become
Christians and put our faith in Christ. The Spirit inspired Scripture, qualifies men for special tasks, and
teaches and guides the Church, leading it in truth.

"The fellowship of the Holy Spirit." *Fellowship*
means companionship. We have fellowship or companionship with all three members of the Trinity: the Father
and the Son (1 John 1:3) and the Holy Spirit (2 Corinthians 13:14).

TOPIC: *II. Knowing God*
SUBTOPIC: *E. God the Holy Spirit*
VERSE: *(2) John 14:26*
> *The Counselor, the Holy Spirit, whom the
> Father will send in my name, will teach
> you all things and will remind you of
> everything I have said to you.*

CONCEPT

The Holy Spirit is sent by God to be our Helper.

COMMUNICATING THE CONCEPT

"Counselor." The meaning of *counselor* as it is used herein referring to the Holy Spirit means someone who comes to our side to help us. The Holy Spirit is a Counselor or Helper (John 14:26, NASB) in many ways to us. He comforts us (John 14), teaches us and guides us in the truth (John 14:26, 16:13), and dwells within us (John 14:17). He gives us whatever help we need to live the Christian life.

"Teach you all things." Jesus promised the disciples that He would continue to teach them all they needed to know through the Holy Spirit.

"Remind you of everything I have said." The Holy Spirit not only continued to teach the disciples; He helped them remember the teachings that Jesus gave them while He was with them. Today the Holy Spirit fulfills the same teaching role in our lives through the Scriptures.

TOPIC: *II. Knowing God*
SUBTOPIC: *E. God the Holy Spirit*
VERSE: *(3) 1 Corinthians 2:12*
We have not received the spirit of the world but the Spirit who is from God, that we may understand what God has freely given us.

CONCEPT

One of the functions of the Holy Spirit in our lives is to help us understand all that is ours as Christians.

COMMUNICATING THE CONCEPT

"Spirit of the world." Paul is emphasizing the source of the Holy Spirit. The Spirit does not come from the world; He comes from God.

"That we may understand." The Holy Spirit helps us understand all the blessings we received when we became Christians. How many can you think of? Paul goes on to tell us in 1 Corinthians 2:14 that a man without the Holy Spirit cannot make sense of or understand spiritual truths.

The man who isn't a Christian can't understand and can't accept these thoughts from God, which the Holy Spirit teaches us. They sound foolish to him, because only those who have the Holy Spirit within them can understand what the Holy Spirit means. Others just can't take it in. (1 Corinthians 2:14, TLB)

TOPIC: *II. Knowing God*
SUBTOPIC: *F. The Spirit in me*
VERSE: *(1) 1 Corinthians 3:16*
*Don't you know that you yourselves are
God's temple and that God's Spirit lives
in you?*

CONCEPT

The Holy Spirit lives in you and me.

COMMUNICATING THE CONCEPT

"Don't you know?" This is a rhetorical question. It is something we should know, but occasionally our behavior betrays the fact that we need to be reminded.

"Temple." In this verse, *temple* means sanctuary or house. Our body is the dwelling place of God.

"God's Spirit lives in you." How did this happen? God's Spirit takes up residence in our lives when we put our faith in Jesus Christ. John Stott very succinctly summarizes this as follows: "We receive the Holy Spirit 'by hearing (the gospel) with faith' (Galatians 3:2) or, more simply still, 'through faith' (Galatians 3:14). As a result, all God's sons possess the Spirit (Galatians 4:6), are led by the Spirit (Romans 8:14), and are assured by the Spirit of their sonship and of God's love (Romans 8:15,16; 5:5)."[3]

What's He doing in us? The Spirit is helping us to be like Christ (2 Corinthians 3:17-18). The big word to describe this process is *sanctification*. Some of the results of His working in our lives are called the "fruit of the

77

Spirit" and are listed in Galatians 5:22-23. This is an upcoming memory passage.

TOPIC: *II. Knowing God*
SUBTOPIC: *F. The Spirit in me*
VERSE: *(2) Romans 8:9*
You, however, are controlled not by the sinful nature but by the Spirit, if the Spirit of God lives in you.

CONCEPT
With the Holy Spirit living in us, our obedience to God is not just dependent on our own strength. The Holy Spirit controls us and gives us the necessary resources to do what is right.

COMMUNICATING THE CONCEPT
"The sinful nature." Here we see that sin is more than a wrong we commit or a good deed we fail to do; it is a part of our nature. Before people become Christians, a sinful nature is the only nature they have. They are totally controlled by it (Ephesians 2:1-3).

Who's driving? Before we became Christians, it's as if we, with our sinful nature, were in the driver's seat controlling the car of our lives. When we come to Christ, the Holy Spirit climbs in the car and says, "Get out of the driver's seat. I'm driving." If we allow Him to drive and control the direction of our "car," we will experience the joy of obedience. If we decide to retake control, there will be wrong turns and negative consequences down the road!

"If the Holy Spirit lives in you." This is a good time to review the previous memory verse (1 Corinthians 3:16) and reinforce understanding.

Who has the Holy Spirit dwelling in them?
When does the Holy Spirit come in to live in us?
What is He doing in us?

TOPIC: *II. Knowing God*
SUBTOPIC: *F. The Spirit in me*
VERSE: *(3) Galatians 5:22-23*
The fruit of the Spirit is love, joy, peace, patience, kindness, goodness, faithfulness, gentleness and self-control.

CONCEPT

When the Holy Spirit lives in you and me and controls us, these character qualities will be seen in our lives.

COMMUNICATING THE CONCEPT

A picture of Christ. The fruit of the Spirit is like a description of Jesus. That's the job of the Spirit as He lives in us: to transform us to be increasingly like Christ.

"Fruit." An apple tree doesn't produce peaches, nor does a pear tree produce cherries! The concept is the same here. People with the Holy Spirit in them produce a certain kind of behavior and character. "No good tree bears bad fruit, nor does a bad tree bear good fruit. Each tree is recognized by its own fruit. . . . The good man brings good things out of the good stored up in his heart, and the evil man brings evil things out of the evil stored up in his heart" (Luke 6:43-45).

Memory aid. Break the fruit into three categories of three. The first three (love, joy, peace) are all one-syllable words. The second three (patience, kindness, goodness) are two-syllable words, and the third group (faithfulness, gentleness, self-control) are all three-syllable words.

NOTES: 1. Garry Friesen, "Painless Scripture Memory," *Moody Monthly*, Volume 82, Number 2, October 1981, page 17.

2. Friesen, "Painless Scripture Memory," page 18.

3. John R.W. Stott, *The Baptism and Fullness of the Holy Spirit* (Downers Grove, Ill.: InterVarsity Press, 1964), page 18.

III. GROWING AS A CHRISTIAN

The Navigator "Wheel Illustration" gives an excellent overview of the topic, "Growing as a Christian."

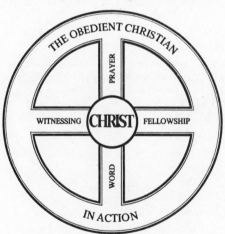

To grow as a Christian requires development in each area represented in the "Wheel." The two vertical spokes, prayer and the Word, are the basis of our relationship with God. The horizontal spokes, witnessing and fellowship, represent our relationship with people. We witness to nonChristians and fellowship with Christians. Jesus is the Center of the wheel. Just as the hub of a wheel provides the power for the wheel to turn, Jesus is the power source in a Christian's life. Having devotions is an excellent way to receive that power. The outer rim, obedience, is the result of the wheel working properly in our lives.

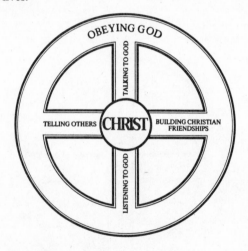

The memory verses in "Growing as a Christian" represent each part of the Wheel Illustration. The titles are changed to reflect the understanding levels of elementary children. The spoke called the Word is now "Listening to God." Prayer has been changed to "Talking to God." Witnessing is "Telling Others." And fellowship is changed to "Building Christian Friendships." Like the other topics, this is action oriented. Having devotions helps keep Christ central in our lives.

REVIEW PLAN
1. The "Understanding Salvation" verses are now well-planted in your child's memory. At this point, you can shift to reviewing them once a week. This should be sufficient to keep these verses sharp and available to the Holy Spirit to bring to mind at appropriate times.
2. Continue to review "Knowing God" daily.
3. As each "Growing as a Christian" verse is memorized, add it to your daily review.

Your child will be able to quote eighteen verses by the end of this main topic. Great!!!

Growth charts. Growth charts are fun. Everyone enjoys seeing progress. You may want to make a Bible memory progress chart to use with this topic. At the top of the chart, put a large ice cream cone or something else that would be motivational and special. As each verse is memorized, mark the progress. When all the verses have been memorized and the ice cream cone is reached, have a celebration!

TOPIC: *III. Growing as a Christian*
SUBTOPIC: *A. Listening to God*
VERSE: *(1) Matthew 4:4*
*"Man does not live on bread alone, but
on every word that comes from the
mouth of God."*

CONCEPT

The concept here is that the Word of God is as essential
for our lives as food itself. It must be a part of our diets in
order for us to be healthy.

COMMUNICATING THE CONCEPT

"Bread." *Bread* is a generic word meaning food, one
of the absolute necessities of life. Jesus says that to live as
God intended, there is another absolute necessity, and
that is the Word of God. Just as physical food helps us
grow physically, so the spiritual food of the Word helps
us grow spiritually. Both kinds of growth are essential.
Look up Jeremiah 15:16. What happened to Jeremiah
as he "ate" the Word of God?

"Why should I memorize the Bible?" This is a
good question. Matthew 4:4 gives us two answers, and
the next two memory verses will add to these reasons.

1. It is evident from this passage that Jesus knew
   Scriptures by heart. In this verse He is quoting
   Deuteronomy 8:3. If it was important and necessary for Him to know this verse by heart, it must
   be even more so for us!

2. Scripture memory keeps us from sin. Because Jesus knew Deuteronomy 8:3, He knew what was right when Satan tempted Him. He had a ready answer. This record is in Matthew 4:1-11.

The power of God's Word. "We should not forget the power of God's word in a child's life even though it doesn't seem to be producing the results we would like to see. Even if our children seem to be rebelling, we can rely on the fact that the seed of Scripture is there for the Holy Spirit to act upon, though it may not be evident to us until many years later."[1]

TOPIC: *III. Growing as a Christian*
SUBTOPIC: *A. Listening to God*
VERSE: *(2) Psalm 119:105*
Your word is a lamp to my feet and a light for my path.

CONCEPT

In this verse we find that Scripture helps us identify the way we should live.

COMMUNICATING THE CONCEPT

In the dark. Imagine yourself needing to hike through a forest on a dark, moonless night. The path you have to take is full of turns, rocks, roots, and often comes close to the edge of a dangerously steep cliff. If you have the choice of taking a flashlight to help you see the path or stumbling around in the dark, which would be the best to do?

Have you ever tried to find your way around in your house on a dark night and bumped into the furniture? A flashlight can keep you from hurting yourself.

The Word of God is like a flashlight to us. It guides us daily by pointing out things that could hurt us and by lighting up the right path. "Your words are a flashlight to light the path ahead of me, and keep me from stumbling" (Psalm 119:105, TLB).

2 Peter 1:19. "We have the word of the prophets made more certain, and you will do well to pay attention to it, *as to a light shining in a dark place.*"

TOPIC: *III. Growing as a Christian*
SUBTOPIC: *A. Listening to God*
VERSE: *(3) Psalm 119:11*
   I have hidden your word in my heart that I might not sin against you.

CONCEPT

Here the writer highlights another important way that the Scriptures help us grow spiritually: by helping us to understand and avoid sin. The process through which this happens is as important to understand as the result.

COMMUNICATING THE CONCEPT

"Hidden." The NASB actually translated this as "Thy word I have treasured in my heart, that I may not sin against Thee." Ask your child to define "treasure," and then ask what we usually do with treasure. We hide it away in a safe place, but a place where we can get to it when we need it. So it is with God's Word. It is a very special treasure, and it needs to be put in a safe place where we can have access to it when we need it. God tells us that this safe place is our hearts!

"Your word." You will want to make sure that it is clearly understood that this phrase refers to the Bible.

"In my heart." The Jews used the word *heart* to define that part of the body that governed all their actions. *The New Bible Dictionary* says that our word "'mind' is perhaps the closest modern term to the biblical usage of 'heart.'"[2] We are to store the Word of God in our mind and allow it to affect all our actions.

"Sin against you." "You" here refers to God. All sin, no matter who we have offended or wronged, even if it is ourselves, is also sin against God. The story of Ananias and Sapphira in Acts 5:1-11 is a clear illustration of this. Peter confronts Ananias and says, "You have not lied to men but to God."

Psalm 37:31. "The law of his God is in his heart; his feet do not slip."

TOPIC: *III. Growing as a Christian*
SUBTOPIC: *B. Talking to God*
VERSE: *(1) John 16:24*

> *"Until now you have not asked for any-thing in my name. Ask and you will receive, and your joy will be complete."*

CONCEPT

God not only wants us to pray; He wants to answer our prayers.

COMMUNICATING THE CONCEPT

"Until now." Jesus was preparing the disciples for His coming death and departure. It was time for them to learn some things about prayer. Until this time ("now") they were able to make requests directly to Jesus. With His upcoming death, they would have to learn to pray to the Father.

"In my name." We approach God and make our requests on the basis of what Jesus has done for us. What is that?

"Your joy will be complete." Be sure to take some time to explain the meaning of joy. Joy is a long-lasting happiness that comes from God. Because it comes from God and not our circumstances, we can be "joyful" even when things around us are not encouraging. When we pray, we will always experience more joy than if we don't. Our joy will be less than full if we cut corners and don't pray.

Memory tip. An effective and fun way to learn a

new verse is to use a blackboard or a computer. Write out the entire verse, including its name and address. After having your "well-versed kid" read it several times, randomly erase two or three words, having him or her supply from memory the missing portions. Continue until you have erased the entire verse and he or she can say it from memory.

TOPIC: *III. Growing as a Christian*
SUBTOPIC: *B. Talking to God*
VERSE: *(2) 1 John 5:14*
> *This is the confidence we have in approaching God: that if we ask anything according to his will, he hears us.*

CONCEPT

Does God answer every prayer? In this verse we have an important guideline regarding our prayers and His answers.

COMMUNICATING THE CONCEPT

A magic key? Prayer is not a magic key that unlocks the door to whatever we want. Prayer is talking to God about your concerns and asking Him what is best.

"Confidence." *Confidence* means assurance. You can be confident or sure that God will hear your prayers.

"According to his will." God hears and answers

our prayers that are according to His will and plan for our lives. John adds in 1 John 5:15, "And if we know that he hears us—whatever we ask—we know that we have what we asked of him." Romans 12:2 lists three qualities of God's will for us: His will is good, pleasing, and perfect. Those are the kind of answers to prayer that He gives us.

What should you do if you don't know God's will? Does that mean you should not ask? No, ask anyway, but tell Him that you want His will. A good illustration of this is Jesus in Matthew 26:39.

Getting started in prayer. Look ahead to the "Application help" under topic VI "Great Bible Truths" A1 (1 John 1:9) for a good method of teaching children how to begin to pray.

TOPIC: *III. Growing as a Christian*
SUBTOPIC: *B. Talking to God*
VERSE: *(3) 1 Thessalonians 5:16-18*
Be joyful always; pray continually; give thanks in all circumstances, for this is God's will for you in Christ Jesus.

CONCEPT

These verses contain three short admonitions, all related to prayer. The two new concepts introduced deal with the regularity of prayer and giving thanks.

COMMUNICATING THE CONCEPT

"Be joyful always." This is a good time to review the concepts in John 16:24. Answered prayer is one key to experiencing the completeness of joy. There is no way we can be fully joyful if we are not regularly praying.

"Pray continually." Continuous prayer is a regular habit of prayer, no matter what the circumstances. If you are a parent, this may be a good point for you to begin, if you have not done so already, to have a regular prayer time with your child. You may want also to begin to encourage other regular prayer habits, such as praying quietly in school, "God, please help me remember what I studied for in this test," etc.

"Give thanks in all circumstances." We are not told to give thanks *for* all circumstances, but to give thanks *in* all circumstances. Make a list of things about God we can be thankful for no matter how bad the situation.

"This is God's will for you." To do these three things is not just a good idea, or Mom and Dad's wish. It's God's will, and so we don't have a choice; they are not optional. The only choice we have is to obey or disobey God. This is true for adults, too!

TOPIC: *III. Growing as a Christian*
SUBTOPIC: *C. Obeying God*
VERSE: *(1) James 1:22*
> *Do not merely listen to the word, and so deceive yourselves. Do what it says.*

CONCEPT

God does desire that we listen to Him. But this is only the first step. The second and more important step is obedience to what we've heard.

COMMUNICATING THE CONCEPT

"Listen." This word represents taking the Scriptures into our mind with our senses. We can do this in a number of ways: by listening to someone teach the Bible, by personally reading it, by doing Bible study, and even by memorizing it. God says this is not enough! To each one of these we need to add obedience. Our goal is not to know more, but to be more like Christ.

Growth requires action. If we are only "listening," we are not growing. Growth requires application and action. This concept of obedience is repeated throughout the Bible.

Jesus taught it—Matthew 7:24-27.
Paul taught it—Romans 2:13.
The psalmist taught it—Psalm 119:4.

Take a step of growth. Don't just be a hearer of this verse; let's put it into action! Together identify one action that both you and your child could take in the next couple of days to do something the Bible says.

A personal testimony from Sue. I was so glad that I had memorized Colossians 3:8-12 on a day when I felt angry with a neighbor. I knew from those verses that anger does not please God, but my feeling was real. Having memorized these verses was not enough; I needed to take action. As I thought about how I could apply each of the adjectives in verse 12 ("Clothe your-selves with compassion, kindness, humility, gentleness and patience") with my neighbor, my feelings of anger quickly evaporated and I could do what was right. Memorizing this passage was a first and necessary step, but I grew when I used the verse to change my attitude.

TOPIC: *III. Growing as a Christian*
SUBTOPIC: *C. Obeying God*
VERSE: *(2) John 14:15*
"If you love me, you will obey what I command."

CONCEPT

Obeying the Bible is a way that we demonstrate that we love Jesus.

COMMUNICATING THE CONCEPT

"If you love me, you will." Love is not a feeling; it is something you do. It shows in your actions and requires a decision to do something. What are some of the things that we do for people that we love? See how many the child can think of. Our love for Jesus Christ is also seen from our actions—obeying His commands.

Obedience and love. These two concepts are tied together many times in the Scriptures. Here are a few verses you could use for devotions to help reinforce this important truth.

John 14:21: "Whoever has my commands and obeys them, he is the one who loves me."

1 John 2:4: "The man who says, 'I know him,' but does not do what he commands is a liar."

Psalm 119:140 (RSV): "Thy promise is well tried, and thy servant loves it."

TOPIC: *III. Growing as a Christian*
SUBTOPIC: *C. Obeying God*
VERSE: *(3) Psalm 119:44*
I will always obey your law, for ever and ever.

CONCEPT

We never outgrow our need to obey the Word of God. It should be a lifelong commitment for us, just as it was for the psalmist.

COMMUNICATING THE CONCEPT

"Law." The Hebrew word for *law* meant teaching. It stood for the revealed will of God. "It is the loving instruction of a parent."[3] It is one of nine words used in Psalm 119 as synonyms for the will of God. Can you find eight more? (statutes, ways, precepts, decrees, commands, word, promises, commandments).

"For ever and ever." Why say it twice? Repetition designates emphasis and importance. It's important that we never stop emphasizing personal obedience. We need to work on it the rest of our lives.

In your own words. To increase and check your child's understanding, have him or her write this verse in his or her own words. This is a helpful exercise whenever you want to reinforce understanding.

TOPIC: *III. Growing as a Christian*
SUBTOPIC: *D. Telling others*
VERSE: *(1) Acts 1:8*

> *"You will receive power when the Holy
> Spirit comes on you; and you will be my
> witnesses in Jerusalem, and in all Judea
> and Samaria, and to the ends of the
> earth."*

CONCEPT

Because we are Christians, we are to be witnesses for
Jesus Christ.

COMMUNICATING THE CONCEPT

**"Receive power when the Holy Spirit comes
on you."** When Jesus broke the news to His disciples
that He was returning to be with the Father, He also told
them of the Counselor who was going to come. They
would exchange Jesus' physical presence for the indwelling of the Holy Spirit, the third Person of the Trinity
(John 14:16-17). Pentecost was the day when this trans-
pired. When the Holy Spirit came on the disciples, they
received power to carry out the task of being witnesses,
which Jesus had left to them. The Holy Spirit gives us the
same power when we become Christians.

I saw it! A witness is a person who has seen or heard
something. He tells what he knows. A Christian witness
tells what he knows about Jesus. In 1 John 1:1-3, the
Apostle John says he is sharing with others what he saw
and heard.

"Jerusalem." Jerusalem is the city where Acts 1:8 was taking place. "Jerusalem" for us is our hometown.

"Judea." Judea was the province in which Jerusalem was located. A province is a large division of a country, much like a state. Canada is divided into provinces instead of states.

"Samaria." North of Judea was the province of Samaria. Not only were the Samaritans citizens of a more distant province; they were people that the Jews did not get along with.

Personalizing Acts 1:8. If you live in Chicago, you could personalize this verse by saying, "Because I have the Holy Spirit, I am a witness in Chicago, in all Illinois and Wisconsin, and to wherever God sends me."

TOPIC: *III. Growing as a Christian*
SUBTOPIC: *D. Telling others*
VERSE: *(2) Mark 5:19*
> *"Go home to your family and tell them how much the Lord has done for you, and how he has had mercy on you."*

CONCEPT

Even though it may often be easier to tell non-family members what it means to be a Christian, we also have a responsibility to share with our own family.

COMMUNICATING THE CONCEPT

"Go home." Jesus had just healed a man who had long been possessed with demons. Many people had tried to help him, but they couldn't. At last, they had given up and let him live like a wild man in the mountains. Finally Jesus healed him. It was only natural that the man wanted to accompany Jesus on His journeys. Jesus told him that his responsibility to tell others began in his "Jerusalem" with his family, and so it was important for the healed man to go home.

A true story. Danny was in the first grade when he memorized the first six "Understanding Salvation" verses. Out to lunch with his grandparents, he asked them to listen to his verses. Grandma and Grandpa were impressed with Danny's memory, but more important, for the first time they didn't make fun of his religion.

You may want to look for a similar situation within your family. Not only will your child have an opportunity to share what he or she has learned about God, but it will be a good review of his or her verses. Repeating Scripture memory verses aloud greatly increases retention.

TOPIC: *III. Growing as a Christian*
SUBTOPIC: *D. Telling others*
VERSE: *(3) Mark 16:15*
"Go into all the world and preach the good news to all creation."

CONCEPT

Not only are we to be witnesses to our families (Mark 5:19), but God has also commanded us as Christians to reach out to all men, wherever they live.

COMMUNICATING THE CONCEPT

Three quotes. All three of the "Telling others" verses are quotes from Christ. They reflect His desire that all men in every place be saved from their sin. Can you think of other statements Jesus made about our responsibility of "telling others"? (Matthew 28:19-20, Luke 24:47-48, John 20:21).

"The good news." This is another phrase for "the gospel." It's good news that Jesus paid the penalty for our sin by His death and resurrection. Perhaps one of the most concise summaries of the good news of the gospel in the New Testament is 1 Corinthians 15:3-4.

But I can't cross the street! It's difficult for a child to envision how he can help take the "good news" into "all the world," but with a little help he can begin to make a significant contribution.

1. He can begin to pray for a missionary family.
2. He can pray for other countries. A globe can help your child identify these countries.
3. He can begin to give to a missionary.

Your local church is a good resource for getting to know missionaries. A missionary family with children about the same age as yours will help your child pray. He can pray for similar things for them that he prays for himself. Try putting a picture of the missionaries on your refrigerator door or other familiar places as a daily reminder.

Three banks. To help set money aside for giving and to teach the three uses of money, set up three banks: a spend bank, a save bank, and a give bank. Agree on a predetermined plan about how your child's allowance and other money will be divided.

TOPIC: *III. Growing as a Christian*
SUBTOPIC: *E. Building Christian friendships*
VERSE: *(1) Hebrews 10:24*
Let us consider how we may spur one another on toward love and good deeds.

CONCEPT

The next three verses on Christian friendship highlight three responsibilities of friendship. The first is that Christian friends need to do more than just enjoy being together. They should help each other be better Christians by encouraging each other to do right.

COMMUNICATING THE CONCEPT

A lettuce verse! Here is a fun memory tip; this verse begins with lettuce ("let us")!

"Consider." This means to take some time to think about something.

"Spur." A cowboy's spur is a pointed little wheel on the back of his boot that he uses to poke or "spur" the horse to get him moving. The meaning is almost the same in this verse. We are to be that spur that helps our friends "get moving," doing things that are helpful and that show love. We all need friends that will spur us!

Well-Versed Kids—a means to the end. "Your heart and the Scriptures were made for each other, and you can tune your inner thoughts and feelings to nothing better than the flawless word of God. With desire and discipline, you can learn by heart passages that the Holy Spirit can use each day to transform your life."[4]

TOPIC: *III. Growing as a Christian*
SUBTOPIC: *E. Building Christian friendships*
VERSE: *(2) Hebrews 3:13*
> *But encourage one another daily, as long as it is called Today, so that none of you may be hardened by sin's deceitfulness.*

CONCEPT

In the last verse we saw that a part of Christian friendship is encouraging each other to do right. Here we see that another aspect is keeping each other from doing wrong.

COMMUNICATING THE CONCEPT

"But" what? The word *but* is a conjunction, an important word connecting words, phrases, or sentences of equal importance. Wherever you see "but" in the Scriptures, it is important to find out what it is connecting. Here it connects a problem in verse 12 with the solution in verse 13. What's the problem? What's the solution?

"Daily." Opportunities to sin surround us every day. We need friends who will give us regular reminders to keep away from sin.

"Hardened." Hard is the opposite of soft or sensitive. A nail will bounce right off a hard piece of steel but will easily go into a soft piece of wood. It's the same with our hearts and God's Word. When we have a hard heart, God's advice and teaching bounces right off and does us no good.

"Sin's deceitfulness." Any pleasure or enjoyment that sin gives is short-lived (Hebrews 11:25). The results of sin always look better than they are.

> Encourage each other every day, while it is still called "today," and beware that none of you becomes deaf and blind to God through the delusive glamour of sin. (Hebrews 3:13, PH)

TOPIC: *III. Growing as a Christian*
SUBTOPIC: *E. Building Christian friendships*
VERSE: *(3) Proverbs 17:17*
A friend loves at all times.

CONCEPT

In this memory verse we have a third characteristic of Christian friendship: unconditional love.

COMMUNICATING THE CONCEPT

Like eternal life. True friendship is like eternal life in two important aspects: it never comes to an end, and it's not dependent upon works. If there is not the commitment to love "at all times," the relationship may be like that described in Proverbs 18:24: "There are friends who pretend to be friends" (RSV).

The Bible is its own best teacher. Discovering other Scriptures that give further insight into a particular verse or subject is an important Bible study skill. There are four basic types of cross-references:

1. Another Scripture that teaches the *same* thing.
2. An *illustration* of the truth.
3. A verse that gives *additional* information.
4. A verse that teaches the truth from the *opposite* perspective.

Below are examples of these four kinds of cross-references to help increase your understanding of Proverbs 17:17. Look them up and discuss them together.

1. John 15:13—teaches the *same* concept.
2. Ruth 1:16, 1 Samuel 19:1-4—an *illustration*.
3. Galatians 6:2—adds *additional* information.
4. Proverbs 19:7—teaches the truth from an *opposite* perspective.

Review. As you review the three verses on "Building Christian friendships," be sure to also review the characteristic of friendship that each verse teaches.

TOPIC: *III. Growing as a Christian*
SUBTOPIC: *F. Having devotions*
VERSE: *(1) Mark 1:35*
Very early in the morning, while it was still dark, Jesus got up, left the house and went off to a solitary place, where he prayed.

CONCEPT

For Jesus, having time to pray was more important than sleeping in after a busy day. He rose early to find a quiet place where He could be alone while He met with His Father.

COMMUNICATING THE CONCEPT

What's the context? Frequently, in order to fully understand a memory verse and allow it to affect our lives as it should, we need to know the context in which it occurs. The context of Mark 1:35 is very important to our appreciation of this verse. Read Mark 1:21-34 and then ask the following questions.

What day was it?
What did Jesus spend His time doing that morning?
    After He left the Synagogue? In the evening?
How many people visited Him after sundown?
How might Jesus have felt at the end of that day?

"Very early in the morning." "Notice how, in spite of the great pressure of work, he was up long before dawn to seek his Father's face—and then ask yourself whether your excuses for omitting a quiet time can ever be valid."[5]

Getting started. Between the ages of ten and thirteen is an appropriate time for a young person to begin to have his own devotions. The Navigator pamphlet *Seven Minutes with God* has been reprinted on pages 191-196 to give some practical ideas on how to start a quiet time.

TOPIC: *III. Growing as a Christian*
SUBTOPIC: *F. Having devotions*
VERSE: *(2) Psalm 5:3*
> *In the morning, O LORD, you hear my*
> *voice; in the morning I lay my requests*
> *before you and wait in expectation.*

CONCEPT

In Mark 1:35 we focused on the *priority* of a quiet time with God. Psalm 5:3 emphasizes *regularity* in our personal devotions.

COMMUNICATING THE CONCEPT

"In the morning . . . in the morning." David chose the morning, every morning, for his personal time with God. Help your child determine what is the best time for him. Then help make that a regular, fixed time every day.

Rewards build regularity. A child will usually begin having a quiet time because someone, usually Mom and Dad, thinks it's a good idea. Personal motivation lags behind. In the interim period, some added external motivation can greatly increase the child's desire to be successful. A weekly chart with a box to check off each day works well. A small reward (such as a dime) for each successful day or a special trip to McDonald's with Dad for a successful week, etc., helps build a consistent pattern while his or her internal motivation and personal conviction catch up with his or her actions. In our spiritual lives, we often begin doing something because someone tells us to. Then we do it because we know it's right. Finally we grow to the point that we do it because we want to.

"I lay my requests before you and wait." *Seven Minutes with God* (pages 191-196) presents an easy and memorable method for prayer: the ACTS prayer plan. An excellent way to encourage looking for God's answers is to keep a prayer list that records both the requests as well as the answers. Have your child keep the list tucked in his Bible so that it's easy to use each day. A sample chart is provided.

REQUEST	ANSWER
1. I could get a job delivering papers.	1. The newspaper called and gave me a job. (8/4)
2. Good fishing on our family vacation.	2. Everyone in our family caught fish everyday.
3. My friend Jim would become a Christian.	3.
4. Dad will have a safe business trip.	4. Home safe!

TOPIC: *III. Growing as a Christian*
SUBTOPIC: *F. Having devotions*
VERSE: *(3) Exodus 33:11*
> *The LORD would speak to Moses face to face, as a man speaks with his friend.*

CONCEPT

As a child's quiet time begins to develop both priority and regularity, a continually growing friendship with the Lord will follow.

COMMUNICATING THE CONCEPT

"The LORD would speak." Spending time in the Scriptures is an important element of our quiet time because this is how God speaks to us today. Good friends discuss a lot of different things together, and so it is with us and God. Time in prayer is us speaking to God. When we read the Word, God is speaking to us.

Ideas for using the Bible in quiet time.

1. Use an inexpensive copy of a version of the Bible that is easily understood, such as the *New International Version*.
2. Start in a book that has a lot of action. The Gospel of Mark would be a good choice.
3. Read one chapter a day.
4. Marking your Bible is a good way to help personalize and remember what God is saying. After reading the chapter through once, reread it with a pencil and mark symbols in the margin.[6]

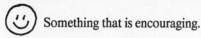 Something that is encouraging.

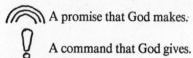 A promise that God makes.

! A command that God gives.

What are other symbols you can use?

NOTES: 1. Bob Seifert, "Scripture Memory for Children," *Discipleship Journal*, Volume 2, Issue 3, May 1982, page 37.

2. J.D. Douglas, ed., *The New Bible Dictionary* (Grand Rapids: Tyndale House Publishers, 1962), pages 509-510.

3. Donald Guthrie, ed., *The New Bible Commentary: Revised* (Grand Rapids: Eerdmans Publishing Company, 1970), page 526.

4. "How to Hide God's Word in Your Heart," *Discipleship Journal*, Volume 2, May 1982, page 33.

5. *Quiet Time—A Practical Guide for Daily Devotions* (Downers Grove, Ill.: InterVarsity Press, 1976), page 3.

6. Terry Hall, *Finally Family Devotions That Work* (Chicago: Moody Bible Institute of Chicago, Moody Press, 1986), used by permission.

IV. ENJOYING GOD

The six subtopics covered in "Enjoying God" represent the six benefits we enjoy because of our relationship with God. The more we grow in our Christian lives, the more we experience these benefits.

"God loves me" and "God cares about me" are foundational truths of the Christian life. Knowing them is the first step to believing them. The youngest elementary child will understand these concepts.

In the third and fourth grades, children are given increasingly more responsibilities. Often the new and unknown lead to new fears. The verses in "God gives me peace" and "God protects me" can be a source of great comfort to this age group.

Two of the struggles of adolescence are dealing with peer pressure and inferiority. Both are real problems for every young person. Memorizing the verses in "God helps me" and "God accepts me" will give your child God's perspective on his or her personal value and worth, as well as provide strength to overcome negative peer pressure.

111

REVIEW PLAN

1. You can now change the "Knowing God" verses from your daily review to your weekly review along with the "Understanding Salvation" verses. It might be helpful to assign a specific day of the week for reviewing each topic.
2. Continue reviewing daily the last main topic, "Growing as a Christian." The first phrase of the verse is key. Emphasize it often.
3. Work on learning one "Enjoying God" verse per week. As it is learned, add it to your daily review. Has your child noticed his verse pack getting fuller and his verse box emptier? PROGRESS!!!

As this topic is completed, again you may want to take one or two weeks off to concentrate on review and application. Now your child can quote twenty-four verses!

Make review fun! Vary it. Instead of reviewing the entire verse each time, quote only the name, address, and first phrase. The first phrase is very important because it's the clue to the entire verse. For another variation, try identifying the main topic and then reading a phrase out of the middle of a verse. See if your child can identify the name and address.

TOPIC: *IV. Enjoying God*
SUBTOPIC: *A. God loves me.*
VERSE: *(1) 1 John 3:16*
> *This is how we know what love is: Jesus Christ laid down his life for us.*

CONCEPT

The best definition and description of love is what God's love is like toward us. The best place to see what love is is Jesus dying for us.

COMMUNICATING THE CONCEPT

Love is giving. Why do we give presents to people at Christmas and on birthdays? Because we love them. When we love someone, we want to give to him. Because God loved us, He gave His Son for us. Jesus loved us and gave up His life for us. Can you help your child think of a verse that says this?

Love without limits. "I'm never going to play with him again!" yelled the angry boy as he stomped into the house. "He's mean. He broke my favorite toy." You've likely heard your child say something similar. Our love for other people often has limits. Many times those limits are related to how they treat us.

God's love for us has no limits. Even though we hurt God by being disobedient, He was willing to have His Son die for us (Romans 5:8). Now that He is our Father and we are His children, His love is still the same. It's not related to how we treat Him.

Love that's the greatest. God wants us to love

113

people the same way: by giving. We are to imitate the love that Christ had for us. "Greater love has no one than this, that he lay down his life for his friends" (John 15:13).

Memory aid. John 3:16 and 1 John 3:16 both talk about God's love: who He loves and how He shows it. These two verses must be "cousins"; they look so much alike they must be from the same family.

TOPIC: *IV. Enjoying God*
SUBTOPIC: *A. God loves me.*
VERSE: *(2) Jeremiah 31:3*
"I have loved you with an everlasting love."

CONCEPT

In this verse, God is reminding His chosen people, the children of Israel, that His love for them will last forever. As Christians, we too are chosen by God. God's love for us as His children will last forever.

COMMUNICATING THE CONCEPT

Our love and God's love. Think with your child about a former favorite toy, perhaps one that he received for Christmas a year or two ago. It was new and shiny, had all its pieces, and worked perfectly. It was loved and many hours were spent playing with it. Now it's probably scratched, has missing pieces, and may not even work. It's just not like it used to be, and neither are your child's feelings about the toy. It rarely gets played with, and another toy has now replaced it as the center of his or her attention.

Thankfully, God's love is not like ours! We may lose interest in things or change friends, but God never loses interest in us. We are always special, always the center of His attention.

"Everlasting." The word *everlasting* means that just as God loved you when He created you, He loves you now, and always will—forever!

TOPIC: *IV. Enjoying God*
SUBTOPIC: *A. God loves me.*
VERSE: *(3) 1 John 4:11*
Dear friends, since God so loved us, we also ought to love one another.

CONCEPT

Because God loves us, our responses should be to love other people. By loving us, God set us free from our sinful, selfish natures. Jesus gave us not only teachings, but also an example to follow so that we'd know what real love is like.

115

COMMUNICATING THE CONCEPT

Me first! God's love for us is one instance where we did *not* make the first move. God loved us as individuals long before we even became aware of Him. That means He loved us before we could earn His love or "un-earn" His love. He simply loves us and always will!

Others second. The fact that God loves us is meant to be more than a warm fuzzy feeling. God's love for us leads to responsibility—loving others. We know how to love others because we have experienced how Jesus loves us.

Review! This is a good time to review the *Well-Versed Kids* verses on God's love (John 3:16, 1 John 3:16, Jeremiah 31:3, 1 John 4:11).

TOPIC: *IV. Enjoying God*
SUBTOPIC: *B. God cares about me.*
VERSE: *(1) 1 Peter 5:7*
Cast all your anxiety on him because he cares for you.

CONCEPT

God cares for us. Because He does, He doesn't want us to do things that are not the best for us. One of those things is worrying.

COMMUNICATING THE CONCEPT

"Cast." We often use this word in fishing. When we throw the fishing line and bait out into the water, we are "casting" it. God wants us to throw or give our worries to Him and leave them there.

How do we do it? Find out the answer in Philippians 4:6-7.

"Anxiety." Anxieties are worries about what might happen. All children have worries. They are afraid of the dark, afraid of thunderstorms, or may be afraid of being left alone. Identify some of the worries that your child has, then talk about them in light of this verse.

Don't assume! Make sure that it is understood that "him" and "he" refer to God.

> Let him have all your worries and cares, for he is always thinking about you and watching everything that concerns you. (1 Peter 5:7, TLB)

TOPIC: *IV. Enjoying God*
SUBTOPIC: *B. God cares about me.*
VERSE: *(2) Nahum 1:7*
The LORD is good, a refuge in times of trouble. He cares for those who trust in him.

CONCEPT

Whether our troubles are worries, fears, or something else, God will care for us if we demonstrate our trust in Him.

COMMUNICATING THE CONCEPT

"Refuge." If an angry, vicious dog is chasing us, we need to take refuge in some place safe, like a house, to protect us. When some kind of trouble is headed our way, we can find the safe refuge that we need in God's protection and care.

"Trust." God's refuge is always there, but we need to demonstrate that we trust or have faith in Him. Praying our memory verse back to God is one of the ways that we do this. For example, you could pray: "Lord, today I am worried about my sister. But I know You are a refuge for me. So right now I choose to trust You with her and not worry. I believe what You said in Nahum 1:7: 'The LORD is good, a refuge in times of trouble. He cares for those who trust in him.'"

A true story. While his parents were away from home, a boy named Scott was hit by a truck and taken to the hospital in serious condition. When his mom heard about the accident, she rushed to the hospital, not knowing if Scott was dead or alive. On the way she quoted Nahum 1:7 over and over again. Repeating the verse helped her to demonstrate her trust in God, and through that trust Scott's mom found tremendous comfort and courage.

By quoting a verse like Nahum 1:7 in a time of

trouble, we affirm that we believe it's true, and are therefore placing our trust in God.

When I am afraid, I will trust in you. (Psalm 56:3)

TOPIC: *IV. Enjoying God*
SUBTOPIC: *B. God cares about me.*
VERSE: *(3) Philippians 4:19*
My God will meet all your needs according to his glorious riches in Christ Jesus.

CONCEPT

The first two memory verses in this topic concentrated on God's care for us when we are worried or in trouble. In Philippians 4:19 we see that God cares about meeting all our needs, no matter what they may be.

COMMUNICATING THE CONCEPT

"My God." Our God is a personal God. He knows the smallest details about us (Matthew 10:30).

Wishes, wants, and needs. Each of us wants more than we need. What are some things we want but probably don't need? God has committed Himself to meet our needs, not our wants. He knows what our needs are (Matthew 6:32) and promises to meet them.

Making it real. For children to learn to look to God as their need-meeter, we must help them identify some of

119

their desires as needs God wants to meet. For example, God created children with a need for social relationships. Perhaps you live in a neighborhood with no other children. Your child will feel the need for friends, but may not naturally think that God wants to help meet that need. By beginning to pray daily with you for that need, he or she will begin to look to God to meet his or her needs. Pray for needs using the guidelines in Colossians 4:2.

"Devote yourselves to prayer . . ." Pray hard! ". . . being watchful . . ." Look for answers! ". . . and thankful." Even before the answers come!

TOPIC: *IV. Enjoying God*
SUBTOPIC: *C. God gives me peace.*
VERSE: *(1) John 14:27*
"Peace I leave with you; my peace I give you. I do not give to you as the world gives. Do not let your hearts be troubled and do not be afraid."

CONCEPT
Peace in our heart can only come from God.

COMMUNICATING THE CONCEPT
"Peace." In the New Testament, peace almost always refers to spiritual peace. First, there must be peace

120

between man and God. The separation and alienation that our sin caused between us and God had to be removed by Christ's sacrifice (Romans 5:1).

The result of peace with God is inward peace. The world can give us pleasure, rest, fun, enjoyment, and possessions. However, the source of all these is outside ourselves. God gives us a peace that comes from within ourselves. This peace originates in our relationship with Him.

When we have peace with God and peace with ourselves, we can then have peace with other people. But first we must do two things: stop doing those things that hurt or harm others, and then begin doing those things that are loving, that make for good relationships and friendships. We will focus on some of these as we begin to memorize the section "Building Character."

Understanding questions. What are the three areas of peace that Jesus makes possible? Why can't we get these anywhere else than from God? How does the peace God gives differ from the world's?

TOPIC: *IV. Enjoying God*
SUBTOPIC: *C. God gives me peace.*
VERSE: *(2) Philippians 4:7*
The peace of God, which transcends all understanding, will guard your hearts and your minds in Christ Jesus.

CONCEPT

You will never totally understand what God's peace is, but you can experience it and enjoy its benefits.

COMMUNICATING THE CONCEPT

"Peace." Some words are easier to define by their opposites. Review the three areas of peace that God gives discussed under John 14:27. What are some words that would describe the opposite of each of these? Worry, frustration, and anxiety might be some.

"Transcends all understanding." *Transcend* will be a new word for many young people, so be sure to take time to define it. Simply, it means to go beyond or above; to be bigger or greater. *The Living Bible* paraphrases it, "far more wonderful than the human mind can understand."

Even though our minds can learn so much and we can understand very complicated things, such as how to build a spaceship, God's peace is something so great and wonderful we will never be able to understand it with our minds. However, the good news is that while we will never understand it, we can experience it. What are other things you don't understand but do experience? For example, how does the picture get to a television screen?

"Will guard your hearts." The context of this verse is important. Philippians 4:6 tells us not to worry about a thing, but to pray, and then we will experience the peace of God. That peace then acts like a guard patrolling the door of our hearts to keep out worries and fears.

Sounds good. How do I get it? Philippians 4:6

gives us the answer: "By prayer . . . present your requests to God." Review 1 Peter 5:7.

TOPIC: *IV. Enjoying God*
SUBTOPIC: *C. God gives me peace.*
VERSE: *(3) 2 Thessalonians 3:16*
Now may the Lord of peace himself give you peace at all times and in every way.

CONCEPT

We can experience the peace we have been learning about at all times and in every circumstance of our lives.

COMMUNICATING THE CONCEPT

"The Lord of peace." Make sure that it is understood that this refers to Jesus. He is the Lord of peace because it is through the Cross that we can have peace with God. Without peace with God as a starting point, there is no real peace of any kind.

"At all times and in every way." This is the key concept in this memory verse. To help make this practical, you may want to discuss the times and situations where your child may not be experiencing God's peace. Take plenty of time to listen and understand. Has he or she been taking the necessary steps to experience peace?

Eye contact. Ross Campbell, in his book *How to Really Love Your Child*, says that eye contact is one of

123

four important ways to communicate "I love you" to your child. Make the most of review sessions by taking the time to make good eye contact.

TOPIC: *IV. Enjoying God*
SUBTOPIC: *D. God protects me.*
VERSE: *(1) Psalm 91:11*
He will command his angels concerning you to guard you in all your ways.

CONCEPT

As children grow, new responsibilities and experiences give rise to new insecurities. These can become new opportunities to experience God's protection.

COMMUNICATING THE CONCEPT

"He will command." Assumption alert! Who is "he"? There are certain things that are very important to God, and the protection of His children is one of them. According to this verse, He did not *ask* the angels to guard us. He *ordered* them to do it!

"In all your ways." God is with us, watching over and protecting us wherever we go. We don't have to worry about God not knowing our location or circumstances.

Psalm 91:11 in action! It was a warm, sunny, summer afternoon in the Colorado Rockies when my son Jeff and I decided to hike up a nearby canyon. We walked for about an hour, crisscrossing a stream before taking a break at a beautiful waterfall. As we were resting, it started to rain lightly. Knowing how fast afternoon storms develop in the mountains, we started to head back down the canyon.

In just a few minutes the light rain changed into blinding torrents, accompanied by thunder, lightening, and hail. As we began to run for fear of a flash flood, a sudden rock slide came crashing down in front of us.

Years before I had memorized Psalm 91:11. And because I had helped Jeff learn it just a few months previously, it was fresh in my mind. How reassuring it was to remember that verse as we were running down the canyon. We were miles from other people, but we knew God was aware of us and able to guard our ways.

TOPIC: *IV. Enjoying God*
SUBTOPIC: *D. God protects me.*
VERSE: *(2) Psalm 91:14*
> *"Because he loves me," says the LORD, "I will rescue him; I will protect him, for he acknowledges my name."*

CONCEPT

Because we are His children (John 1:12), God has already made the decision to protect us.

COMMUNICATING THE CONCEPT

"Because he loves me." The "he" in this verse is not the same as the "he" in the previous verse. In this verse, God is talking. Why not act Psalm 91:14 out for your child, pretending you are God. Say the verse out loud as you act.

"I will . . . I will." This is a promise! The Lord doesn't say "I might" or "I'll think about it." He says, "I *will*."

"Acknowledges my name." To "acknowledge my name" is to believe and accept as true all that God's name represents.

Devotional idea. All of Psalm 91 deals with the subject of God's protection. You may want to read and discuss the entire psalm.

Review. What else can we learn about God's protection from the "God cares about me" verses?

TOPIC: *IV. Enjoying God*
SUBTOPIC: *D. God protects me.*
VERSE: *(3) Psalm 121:7*
*The LORD will keep you from all harm—
he will watch over your life.*

CONCEPT

The Lord is watching over us and will keep us from harm.

COMMUNICATING THE CONCEPT

No harm—ever? Well, maybe! It depends on who is defining what is harmful for us—God or us! There may be things that we think are harmful, but God knows in the long run that they are for our best. His thoughts are not always our thoughts (Isaiah 55:8), but we are assured that His plans for our lives are always for our best (Jeremiah 29:11).

A Scripture memory challenge! All of Psalm 121 is about God's protection and it's worth memorizing. Psalm 121:1-2 will be memorized next in *Well-Versed Kids*, so memorizing the entire psalm will provide an extra challenge, give a head start on future memory work, and help put two of the memory verses into their context.

TOPIC: *IV. Enjoying God*
SUBTOPIC: E. God helps me.
VERSE: (1) Psalm 121:1-2

> I lift up my eyes to the hills—where does my help come from? My help comes from the LORD, the Maker of heaven and earth.

CONCEPT

The psalmist is giving a testimony about God. He knew that God was always there to help him. Since God is the

127

Maker of Heaven and earth, He is powerful enough to give us whatever help we need.

COMMUNICATING THE CONCEPT

"I lift up my eyes to the hills." It is possible that this psalm was written by someone—perhaps a shepherd—who was fearing the dangers of a trip through the mountains, where animals or robbers might suddenly attack or dangerous storms might hit. As he looked to those hills, he realized that he would need protection and help, so he asked, "Who will get me through safely?"

Seeing, smelling, and hearing it! Meditating, or prolonged thinking about a certain portion of Scripture, helps the Bible come alive to us. We begin to see applications for ourselves as Christians. One method of meditation is to put yourself in the place of one of the people in Scripture. Think how you would have felt as the psalmist ready to leave on a trip through the mountains.

What might you see that would cause you to
worry?
What would you hear that frightens you?
What smells are present?
What would you feel that causes anxiety?

"My help comes from the LORD." Why would the Lord want to help us? What are some characteristics of God that would make Him able to help us? How might His help differ from man's help? List some ways in which God might have helped this psalmist.

TOPIC: *IV. Enjoying God*
SUBTOPIC: *E. God helps me.*
VERSE: *(2) Isaiah 41:10*
"Do not fear, for I am with you; do not be dismayed, for I am your God. I will strengthen you and help you; I will uphold you with my righteous right hand."

CONCEPT

Psalm 121:1-2 is man's testimony about God. Isaiah 41:10 is God's testimony about Himself.

COMMUNICATING THE CONCEPT

"Do not fear." Fear is a common emotion, from the youngest child to the oldest adult. It is an uneasy feeling produced by actual, potential, or imagined danger.

"I am with you." The presence of another person often reduces our fear and increases our courage. Remember, when you were a preschooler, how comforting it was to climb in bed with your mom and dad? God is always with His children. Hebrews 13:5 reminds us, "Never will I leave you; never will I forsake you."

"Dismayed." To be dismayed means to be worried, fearful, or discouraged.

"I will strengthen you." God is more than just with us. He gives us strength—all the strength we need to do what is needed, right, and pleasing to Him. Young people will face many hard situations, such as negative peer pressure. If these youngsters are left to their own

129

strength, many situations will overwhelm them. A key to helping young people successfully deal with tough situations is to teach them where their strength lies and where to go for help.

"I will uphold you." Instead of giving in because of fear and lack of personal strength, we can count on God to help us stand firm.

Pray the promises. Remind your child that Scripture memory is not an end in itself. It provides ammunition for the battle. When help is needed, we can quote this verse, and ask God to provide the help and strength He promises.

TOPIC: *IV. Enjoying God*
SUBTOPIC: *E. God helps me.*
VERSE: *(3) Philippians 4:13*
I can do everything through him who gives me strength.

CONCEPT

In whatever situation, God is there to provide help. We must recognize our constant need for His help.

COMMUNICATING THE CONCEPT

"Everything"? Will God help me get an "A" on a test I didn't study for? Make the ball team if I didn't practice? Run faster than a car? Obviously, no! But doesn't "everything" mean *everything*? Sorry, it doesn't! It means I can do everything that is the will of God for me to do. I can be the kind of person He wants me to be. I can do what He wants me to do. He will always give me enough strength to obey.

Who's "him"? "Him" here refers to Jesus Christ. Paul said that Jesus told him, "My power shows up best in weak people." So Paul decided, "Now I am glad to boast about how weak I am; I am glad to be a living demonstration of Christ's power, instead of showing off my own power and abilities" (2 Corinthians 12:9, TLB).

TOPIC: *IV. Enjoying God*
SUBTOPIC: *F. God accepts me.*
VERSE: *(1) Psalm 139:13*
You created my inmost being; you knit me together in my mother's womb.

CONCEPT

God began His work in our lives long before we were born. He is the one who determined each detail of our physical, intellectual, and emotional selves while we were in our mothers' wombs.

COMMUNICATING THE CONCEPT

Something new! With this topic, *Well-Versed Kids* introduces a new type of memory work: memorizing a short passage of Scripture instead of individual verses. All three memory assignments for "God accepts me" will be from Psalm 139:13-16.

Something old! There is an old problem that almost every young person faces: the problem of *inferiority*. Dr. James Dobson, in his book *Preparing for Adolescence*, defines inferiority as "that awful awareness that nobody likes you, that you are not as good as other people, that you're a failure, a loser, a personal disaster; that you're ugly, or unintelligent, or don't have as much ability as someone else."[1] He goes on to say that approximately "80 percent of the teenagers in our society don't like the way they look."[2]

I'm not a mistake. You and I are not products of chance. Rather, God created us just the way He wanted. We are the personal handiwork of God!

"Inmost being." This phrase refers to our psychological part: how we think, how we act, how we feel, how we respond to life.

"You knit me together." God put together our physical nature: our coordination, our height, our features, etc.

TOPIC: *IV. Enjoying God*
SUBTOPIC: *F. God accepts me.*
VERSE: *(2) Psalm 139:14*
> *I praise you because I am fearfully and wonderfully made; your works are wonderful, I know that full well.*

CONCEPT

We are to be thankful for how God created us. He doesn't create junk! He made us exactly as He wants us.

COMMUNICATING THE CONCEPT

"I praise you." Every young person probably ought to include this on his or her daily prayer list! Self-acceptance is a problem for almost everyone, and praising God each day for how He made us will help change our attitudes.

"Your works are wonderful, I know that full well." We need to keep reviewing and repeating the truth of this verse until we believe it deep down inside, until "my soul knows it very well" (NASB). There still may come times when we don't *feel* like this is true, but we *know* it is.

Old tapes—new tapes. Imagine a tape recorder in your mind. For years your bad thoughts have been like listening to a tape filled with lies: "You're no good; people don't like you; you're not good looking"; etc. We need to change tapes and listen over and over to one filled with truth: "Your works are wonderful." Romans 12:2 tells us that transformation comes not through renewing our feelings, circumstances, or our behavior, but by renewing our minds.

TOPIC: *IV. Enjoying God*
SUBTOPIC: *F. God accepts me.*
VERSE: *(3) Psalm 139:15-16*

> *My frame was not hidden from you when I was made in the secret place. When I was woven together in the depths of the earth, your eyes saw my unformed body. All the days ordained for me were written in your book before one of them came to be.*

CONCEPT

God not only created me, but He also planned all my days.

COMMUNICATING THE CONCEPT

"The depths of the earth." This phrase may refer to the fact that the earth is far below Heaven. This makes God's knowledge of us even more amazing.

"All the days ordained for me." God doesn't create us and then just send us off to live life and see what happens. The Bible teaches us that He has numbered our days; we can't add to them. "Who of you by worrying can add a single hour to his life?" (Matthew 6:27). He has not only numbered our days, but He also has a plan for them. "'For I know the plans I have for you,' declares the LORD, 'plans to prosper you and not to harm you, plans to give you hope and a future'" (Jeremiah 29:11).

"In your book." This phrase refers to God's unchanging records.

NOTES: 1. James Dobson, *Preparing for Adolescence* (Ventura, Calif.: Vision House, 1978), page 16.
   2. Dobson, *Preparing for Adolescence*, page 21.

IV. ENJOYING GOD

V. BUILDING CHARACTER

God is not satisfied that we merely know the right things; He wants us to be the right people. We can know a lot about Christ without ever becoming Christlike. Godly character takes a lifetime to develop, but it starts when we are children. Children who have memorized God's expectations for their character have the necessary resources for the Holy Spirit to use to change their lives. "And as the Spirit of the Lord works within us, we become more and more like him" (2 Corinthians 3:18, TLB).

REVIEW PLAN

1. As you start memorizing "Building Character," you may now add the topic "Growing as a Christian" to your "Knowing God" and "Understanding Salvation" verses, which are on a weekly review system. A possible review plan may look like this:

   Monday—Review "Understanding Salvation"
   Tuesday—Review "Knowing God"

Wednesday—Review "Growing as a Christian"
2. Your most recent main topic, "Enjoying God," should still be reviewed daily.
3. Learn one new "Building Character" verse a week and add it to your daily review.

At the end of this topic, your child will be able to quote thirty key Bible passages. That is fantastic! Keep it up.

As you review and memorize, remember that retention is more important than new learning. Encourage and help your child to learn the verses well, to be truly a well-versed kid.

TOPIC: *V. Building Character*
SUBTOPIC: *A. Be obedient to parents.*
VERSE: *(1) Ephesians 6:1*
*Children, obey your parents in the Lord,
for this is right.*

CONCEPT

It is God's plan that children obey their parents, and this obedience is right.

COMMUNICATING THE CONCEPT

"In the Lord." This phrase denotes the sphere or context in which the action of obedience is taking place. In other words, obedience to parents is more than just obeying parental authority. It also falls in the arena of spiritual duty. When a child obeys his parents, he is obeying the Lord. Children should obey not only because they love their parents, but also because they respect and love Jesus Christ.

"For this is right." Ask your "well-versed kid" why he or she obeys or should obey Mom and Dad. You may be surprised at the answers! Reinforce the idea that obedience is "right," and that obedience pleases God. This is an excellent time to preview the verses and concepts under II-C, "Obeying God."

Memory tip. Acting out verses makes the initial work of memory not only fun but also easier, particularly if you are working with a small group of kids. Have them work together for a few minutes to plan actions for the verse and then let them present their version.

A note for teachers. You may have some children in your class from nonChristian homes. These children may need extra instruction. Children should always obey their parents *except* if their parents ask them to disobey God's Word—for instance, if parents would ask their child to lie. If this happens, the Bible has the higher authority. Look ahead to the notes for the next memory verse.

TOPIC: *V. Building Character*
SUBTOPIC: *A. Be obedient to parents.*
VERSE: *(2) Colossians 3:20*
Children, obey your parents in everything, for this pleases the Lord.

CONCEPT

In the previous memory verse, we primarily emphasized the reason for obedience. In this verse the emphasis is on the extent of that obedience: "in everything."

COMMUNICATING THE CONCEPT

"In everything"? There are limitations on this. One is given to us in Acts 5:29: "We must obey God rather than men." Perhaps the underlying principle is that all authority is limited. A husband doesn't have the authority to tell his wife to drive 80 mph in a 35 mph speed zone. An employer doesn't have authority over an employee's family. If parents transgress the bounds of their legitimate authority, then obedience is not required.

Time out for parents! Paul balanced this command to children with an admonition to parents: "Fathers, do not embitter your children, or they will become discouraged" (Colossians 3:21). To embitter means to "exasperate" (NASB).

As parents, if our expectations are too great and are beyond our children's capacities to fulfill, then our children will become frustrated, which will lead to discouragement. When discouragement has run its course, it winds up in bitterness and rebellion.

On the positive side, "One of the most powerful motivating forces available to parents [is] praise."[1] One idea to help you praise your child is to use a special plate only at certain mealtimes. Use it for any reason you can think of: an "A" on a test, a goal scored in a soccer game, a birthday, or for no reason at all except to say "You are special!"

TOPIC: *V. Building Character*
SUBTOPIC: *A. Be obedient to parents.*
VERSE: *(3) Proverbs 1:8*
Listen, my son, to your father's instruction and do not forsake your mother's teaching.

CONCEPT

Walking in the way of obedience requires that a child know what that way is. One of the best sources to learn that way is through the instruction and teaching of Mom and Dad.

COMMUNICATING THE CONCEPT

"Listen." It is likely that *listen* here means more than just hear with the ear. It includes translating the instruction and teaching what was heard with the ear into action. When we listen to God, we are to listen with the intent to obey. James 1:22 will be memorized later and will give additional insight.

It takes more than Scripture memory! Instructing, teaching, and helping our children memorize the Word is important, but it leaves out one essential ingredient: prayer. Writing about Dawson Trotman, the founder of The Navigators, Betty Skinner recalls his nonChristian teenage years: "The verses of Scripture he had diligently memorized, not for spiritual profit but for the sake of competition, took root. The prayers of a mother, a neighbor, and two concerned teachers could be answered now that the Holy Spirit had wherewith to work—the incorruptible seed."[2]

TOPIC: *V. Building Character*
SUBTOPIC: *B. Be honest.*
VERSE: *(1) Leviticus 19:11*
   Do not steal. Do not lie. Do not deceive one another.

CONCEPT

Three facets of dishonesty are introduced in this verse: stealing, lying, and deceiving.

COMMUNICATING THE CONCEPT

Stealing. Stealing is to take something that belongs to someone else. When we steal from one another, we not only sin against the other person, Proverbs 30:9 says that stealing is also a sin against God because it dishonors His name. Why is that?

Lying. Lying is simply not telling the truth. Read the story of Ananias and Sapphira in Acts 5:1-11 and see how they lied to Peter and the other apostles. Who did they sin against? How seriously does God take lying?

Deceiving. To deceive somebody is to cause him to believe something that isn't true. It may involve lying, or it may not. It could even involve telling the truth, but perhaps not the whole truth.

A stolen basketball. We printed our last name in big black letters on our son's brand new basketball. One evening the kids were careless and left the ball lying in the front yard. The temptation was too great for a little neighbor girl and the ball went dribbling home with her. There she cleverly changed our last name into her first name! If at that point her mom had asked her, "Is that your ball?" she could have honestly replied, "Look, it has my name on it." She would not have lied, but would have been deceitful.

TOPIC: *V. Building Character*
SUBTOPIC: *B. Be honest.*
VERSE: *(2) Colossians 3:9*
Do not lie to each other, since you have taken off your old self with its practices.

CONCEPT

Leviticus 19:11 taught three facets of honesty. Colossians 3:9 teaches us why we need to be honest.

COMMUNICATING THE CONCEPT

Old self—new self. Second Corinthians 5:17 says that when we become a Christian, we are transformed into a *new* person, and as a result, "The old has gone, the new has come."

Old father—new Father. When we become Christians, we not only become new creations (2 Corinthians 5:17), but we also receive a new Father. John 8:44 states that Satan is our old father and his natural language is lying, "for he is a liar and the father of lies." Our new Father is characterized by truth: "I, the LORD, speak the truth; I declare what is right" (Isaiah 45:19).

Old practices—new practices. When we were our old selves, aligned with our old father, we had some old practices. Colossians 3:7-9 gives us a list. These old practices don't fit with our new selves and our new Father. We need to discard them, just like a shirt that doesn't fit because we have outgrown it.

TOPIC: *V. Building Character*
SUBTOPIC: *B. Be honest.*
VERSE: *(3) Acts 24:16*
I strive always to keep my conscience clear before God and man.

CONCEPT

In the previous verses we have looked at the importance of honesty. Now we will look at what we need to do when we make a mistake or do something wrong.

COMMUNICATING THE CONCEPT

What's a clear conscience? A clear conscience comes from knowing that there is no wrong you have done, either toward God or man, for which you have not asked forgiveness. It's knowing that "no one can point a finger at you and say, 'You've offended me, and you've never asked my forgiveness.'"[3]

"I strive always." The RSV says, "I always take pains to have a clear conscience." Having a clear conscience is not easy. Asking forgiveness is hard and often painful. Yet no matter how hard or painful it may be, we are to make every effort to have a clear conscience.

How not to do it! When it comes to asking forgiveness, we try to make it less painful by never really asking for forgiveness. Bill Gothard gives the following examples:

"I was wrong, but you were too."
"I'm sorry about it, but it wasn't all my fault."
"I'm sorry."
"If I've been wrong, please forgive me."[4]

The hardest yet most necessary statement is, "Will you please forgive me?"

If forgiveness has been granted, the offended person will not (1) bring the incident up again with the offender, (2) bring the incident up to others, or (3) stew over it himself.

TOPIC: *V. Building Character*
SUBTOPIC: *C. Be dependable.*
VERSE: *(1) Numbers 23:19*
"God is not a man, that he should lie, nor a son of man, that he should change his mind. Does he speak and then not act? Does he promise and not fulfill?"

CONCEPT

The goal of our character growth is always godliness. As we begin this topic of dependability, our first memory verse highlights the fact that dependability is characteristic of God.

COMMUNICATING THE CONCEPT

Dependability. Dependability is a character trait with two key elements: first, you can be counted on to do what you say; second, you can be counted on to always do what is right.

Why are there no answers? It may be necessary to define what a rhetorical question is. A rhetorical question is asked to emphasize what everyone knows to be true and therefore it does not need to be answered. What are some other rhetorical questions? What are the answers to the two in this verse?

The character of God. Using the information in Numbers 23:19, make a list of God's characteristics. If we thought that God lied and didn't keep His promises, would we trust Him? If we desire people to trust us, then we need to build these same characteristics into our lives.

TOPIC: *V. Building Character*
SUBTOPIC: *C. Be dependable.*
VERSE: *(2) Luke 16:10*

> *"Whoever can be trusted with very little can also be trusted with much, and whoever is dishonest with very little will also be dishonest with much."*

CONCEPT

Dependability is a character trait that is learned and developed in the small areas of our lives.

COMMUNICATING THE CONCEPT

"Little . . . much." Here Jesus is giving us a basic truth about man: character cannot be compartmentalized. What is true in the minor areas of our lives carries over to the major areas. This verse may also be telling us that character is most easily seen in the little things. Whatever is true of the little things will be true of the other areas of our lives. Discuss what some of the little areas are in your child's life where he or she can learn to be dependable.

Chores? Around our house two of the training grounds for dependability are daily chores and Saturday jobs. Our sons think they do them to *earn* their allowance, but actually they do them to *learn* dependability, serving, responsibility, excellence, and hard work.

Is Bible memory one of those little things? Most children do not realize the importance of Bible memory. They are doing it because of a parent's or teacher's desire, or the short-term rewards. To them Bible memory is a "little thing." Use the example of Bible memory to teach your child the correlation between little and big things.

TOPIC: *V. Building Character*
SUBTOPIC: *C. Be dependable.*
VERSE: *(3) Proverbs 28:20*
A faithful man will be richly blessed.

CONCEPT

Growth in any character area of our lives is not easy. It's the result of prayer and a determined effort to walk in obedience. God will always bless the person who lives obediently. John 14:21 lists one of the greatest blessings of obedience: "Whoever has my commands and obeys them, he is the one who loves me. He who loves me will be loved by my Father, and I too will love him and show myself to him."

COMMUNICATING THE CONCEPT

Blessings of faithfulness. Matthew 25:14-30 contains a parable about faithfulness and unfaithfulness. Read this parable as a family. What were the rewards for the faithful men? Read Proverbs 28:19 as another good example of the blessed results of dependability. Discuss some examples from around your house

149

that illustrate how dependability was or will be rewarded.

A bad tooth! Do people enjoy being around some-one who's not dependable? They probably enjoy it about as much as they enjoy having a sore tooth! Proverbs 25:19 compares the unfaithful person to a bad tooth. When you have a sore tooth, the tooth doesn't keep its pain to itself. It shares its hurt with you! The undependable person is just like that tooth. He does more than harm himself; he disappoints and hurts other people.

TOPIC: *V. Building Character*
SUBTOPIC: *D. Be a servant.*
VERSE: *(1) Mark 10:45*
"Even the Son of Man did not come to be served, but to serve."

CONCEPT

Just as we learned that dependability is a characteristic of God, we begin this topic with the same foundational truth: God is a servant and we are to be imitators of God (Ephesians 5:1). This time we look at Christ for our example and motivation.

COMMUNICATING THE CONCEPT

"The Son of Man." Jesus often referred to Himself as the "Son of Man." You can find an explanation of this phrase in the discussion of Matthew 24:44 under the topic of "Great Bible Truths" VI, C2.

"Did not come to be served." If we could imagine anyone deserving to be served, it would be Jesus. Yet He modeled for us that there is something greater than being served: serving others. "The Lord Jesus himself said: 'It is more blessed to give than to receive'" (Acts 20:35).

Review, review, review. This is an excellent time to review "Understanding Salvation" and reinforce how Jesus served us.

Putting it into practice. Using the word *SERVE* as an acrostic, together with your child come up with five ways that he or she can serve over the next couple of weeks. Check off the items when each project has been completed. Here's an example:

Send Grandma a letter saying you will mow her lawn when you visit her next week.

Encourage Dad by sweeping the garage.

Rake up the leaves in the yard.

Visit our elderly neighbor at her home. Bring her a new magazine.

Examine our living room. Can you help keep it neater?

TOPIC: *V. Building Character*
SUBTOPIC: *D. Be a servant.*
VERSE: *(2) Ephesians 6:7*
Serve wholeheartedly, as if you were serving the Lord, not men.

CONCEPT

Mark 10:45 emphasized why we serve. Our motivation is to be like Christ. In this memory verse on being a servant, we add *how* and *who* we are to serve.

COMMUNICATING THE CONCEPT

"Wholeheartedly." To do something wholeheartedly is to do it the best you can, with all the enthusiasm and energy you have. We are to serve with a good attitude and work hard at it! As Christians, we are to be wholehearted in whatever we do. "Whatever you do, work at it with all your heart, as working for the Lord, not for men, since you know that you will receive an inheritance from the Lord as a reward. It is the Lord Christ you are serving" (Colossians 3:23-24).

But why? "Why do I need to work hard and enthusiastically at serving? I can think of other things that are a lot more fun!" Good question! Here are three good answers:

1. God tells us to!
2. Ephesians 6:8 (the verse that follows this one) tells us that the Lord will reward us for doing good.

3. When we serve others, we are serving the Lord. Matthew 25:34-40 and Colossians 3:24 are excellent references on this concept.

TOPIC: *V. Building Character*
SUBTOPIC: *D. Be a servant.*
VERSE: *(3) Matthew 20:26*
"Whoever wants to become great among you must be your servant."

CONCEPT

In the previous verses on servanthood, we looked at why we serve, how we are to serve, and who we are to serve. Now we look at the results of being a servant.

COMMUNICATING THE CONCEPT

"Instead." To fully understand this verse, you will want to read the context in which it occurs, beginning with verse 20. Matthew 20:26 is the second part of Jesus' summary conclusion. In the first part He says that it is common to think that leaders are not servants—that they should not serve but have people serve them. Jesus says that this is wrong, that real leadership is serving others. Servanthood is not the means to becoming great; it *is* greatness.

Children do what you inspect, not what you expect. Our role as parents in *Well-Versed Kids* is very important to the success of our children. Luke 6:40 reminds us that our children are going to be like us. Remember to plan time daily to help and encourage your children as they become "well-versed kids."

"Among you it is quite different. Anyone wanting
to be a leader among you must be your servant.
And if you want to be right at the top, you must
serve like a slave." (Matthew 20:26-27, TLB)

TOPIC: *V. Building Character*
SUBTOPIC: *E. Be loving.*
VERSE: *(1) 1 Corinthians 13:4*
*Love is patient, love is kind. It does not
envy, it does not boast, it is not proud.*

CONCEPT
Paul wrote the classic scriptural definition of love in 1 Corinthians 13:4-7. To get a feel for the importance of love, discuss Matthew 22:36-40 and 1 Corinthians 13:1-3.

COMMUNICATING THE CONCEPT
It is—it isn't! As you memorize your way through this passage, you may want to make two lists: one which defines what love is, and the other with descriptions of what love is not. Be sure to define and illustrate each

word as you work through this verse and the ones following from this passage.

"Patient." To be a patient person is to be slow in becoming angry with people. We should be patient, not just with our friends, but with everyone! (See 1 Thessalonians 5:14.)

"Kind." Kindness is doing good things for people. Motivating children to be kind is important because kindness is something that can be initiated by the child anytime, or anyplace. Whereas patience is a reaction, kindness is an action. The staff at our sons' school works at cultivating kindness by having a weekly "Kindness Award" that is presented by the principal.

"Envy." Envy is wishing you had what another has. It means to be jealous. Rather than wanting what other people have, love prompts us to be glad they have it. We rejoice with them.

"Boast." Boasting is stretching the truth (that is, lying) so that you or perhaps something you have appears better than it really is. What are some examples? Boasting doesn't fit in with love because it draws attention to ourselves, and love is always other-centered. Love wants the other person to be a success.

"Proud." Proud people are always thinking about themselves. They are usually talking about themselves, and they think they are better than others. What are some ways you have seen people exhibit pride? James 4:6 says, "God opposes the proud but gives grace to the humble." Why is pride not a characteristic of love?

TOPIC: *V. Building Character*
SUBTOPIC: *E. Be loving.*
VERSE: *(2) 1 Corinthians 13:5*
[Love] is not rude, it is not self-seeking, it is not easily angered, it keeps no record of wrongs.

CONCEPT

The description of love in 1 Corinthians 13:4-7 is similar to a sandwich. All the negatives are sandwiched between the positives. Illustrations of what love is *not* are found in 1 Corinthians 13:5.

COMMUNICATING THE CONCEPT

"**Rude.**" The word *rude* has a very broad meaning. It basically means anything that is inappropriate, disgraceful, dishonorable, or indecent. This type of behavior hurts another person, whereas love wants what is best for another. "Love has good manners" (PH).

"**Self-seeking.**" To be *self-seeking* is to busy yourself with your own interests rather than those of others. Philippians 2:3-4 tells us to consider others more important than ourselves and to be involved in their interests as well as ours.

"**Easily angered.**" Hasty anger is the opposite of the patience we discussed in the last verse. J. B. Phillips paraphrases this, "Love . . . is not touchy."

"**No record of wrongs.**" Love always forgives and forgets. Our model for this is God Himself. He has promised that He will always forgive us if we ask for forgiveness (1 John 1:9). When God forgives, He erases all thoughts of our sin from His mind. We are to forgive in the same way (Colossians 3:13). How can we tell if we are keeping a record of someone's wrongs?

TOPIC: *V. Building Character*
SUBTOPIC: *E. Be loving.*
VERSE: *(3) 1 Corinthians 13:6-7*
Love does not delight in evil but rejoices with the truth. It always protects, always trusts, always hopes, always perseveres.

CONCEPT

These two verses end the negatives and provide the other piece of bread for the sandwich!

COMMUNICATING THE CONCEPT

"Does not delight in evil." We are not to be glad when someone does something that is wrong. An evil deed hurts the person who does it, it hurts others, and it hurts Jesus Christ. Why would this be the opposite of love?

"Rejoices with the truth." In 2 Thessalonians 2:10, Paul uses the word *truth* as the opposite of the word *evil*. Love rejoices in the things of God, those things that are true and right.

"Always protects." A possible meaning here is

157

that love does not advertise the weaknesses or problems of another person. Proverbs 17:9 tells us, "He who covers over an offense promotes love, but whoever repeats the matter separates close friends."

"Always trusts." James Moffatt translated this phrase as "always eager to believe the best." It is always easy to think the worst of someone, to quickly accuse him and then not believe him when he says he's innocent. Love should always be ready to "believe the best."

"Always hopes." With love, no failure has to be final. There can always be another chance.

"Always perseveres." Love is never overwhelmed, it doesn't give up, "it endures everything" (AMP).

God is love. John said, "God is love" (1 John 4:8). Since God is love, these verses in 1 Corinthians 13 also describe the character of God, who is our best example of love.

TOPIC: *V. Building Character*
SUBTOPIC: *F. Be committed.*
VERSE: *(1) Romans 12:1*
Therefore, I urge you, brothers, in view of God's mercy, to offer your bodies as living sacrifices, holy and pleasing to God—this is your spiritual act of worship.

CONCEPT

In the following three verses, we will be looking at three successive steps in being committed to the lordship of Jesus Christ. The first, outlined in Romans 12:1, is the step of *surrender*.

COMMUNICATING THE CONCEPT

"Therefore . . . in view of God's mercy." In Scripture whenever you see a "therefore," you want to see what it's "there for." This *therefore* is there for the reason of summarizing all the contents of Romans 1-11. These eleven chapters are a detailed presentation of the gospel. When Paul summarizes this presentation, he uses one term, "God's mercy." He then goes on to add that, in light of all God has done for you, you need to do something.

What's the difference? Here are good definitions of mercy and grace that are simple and easy to remember.

Mercy—God's love in the midst of our failure.
Grace—God's love in the midst of our weakness.

"Offer your bodies." The word *offer* means to make a clear, decisive presentation. Imagine that I have ten dollars in my hand and I say to you, "Would you like ten dollars?" You respond, "Yes!" I give you the ten dollars saying, "Here, I give this to you." I then very clearly and decisively give you the money. We are to do the same thing with God: make a clear and decisive presentation of ourselves to God. "Lord, I give You my body—to use anyway You want—for the rest of my life."

The word *bodies* does not refer to your personality, spirit, gifts, ideas, etc. It refers to *you*! Not your talents, not your money, not your ideas, not your time, but *you*. When God has *you*, He has everything else. God is not hard up for ideas or money, but He does have difficulty finding surrendered people who will carry out His ideas.

God is not limited by our disability.
God is not assisted by our ability.
God wants our availability.

"Living sacrifice." This phrase is a sharp contrast to the dead sacrifices of the Old Testament. God doesn't want some little gift. He wants us. God is asking us to surrender, not just once, but day after day until we see Him face to face.

"Holy." We are to be a particular type of sacrifice: one that is holy. *Holy* means to be set apart, free from defect and blemish, separated from anything that contaminates.

"Your spiritual [or reasonable] act of worship." On the basis of who you are and what Christ has done for you, what Paul spells out in this verse is a reasonable request.

TOPIC: *V. Building Character*
SUBTOPIC: *F. Be committed.*
VERSE: *(2) Romans 12:2*
> *Do not conform any longer to the pattern of this world, but be transformed by the renewing of your mind. Then you will be able to test and approve what God's will is—his good, pleasing and perfect will.*

CONCEPT

The second step of commitment involves a willing and purposeful change in our behavior. We willingly resist conforming to the world's style, and purposefully pursue knowing and doing what is right.

COMMUNICATING THE CONCEPT

Conformed versus transformed. To be conformed to the world is to put on a style of living that comes from the external environment around us and does not reflect our true inner nature as a child of God. It is like wax being shaped by heat. What are some values we can be influenced by that would not be appropriate for a Christian?

To be transformed means that our values have changed to reflect what's inside of us, the Spirit of God. That transformation begins with the renewing of our minds with the Word of God. Whatever fills our thoughts and controls our minds determines what we do.

"Test and approve." To *test and approve* does not mean to determine if the will of God is good or not. It is "to find out or learn by experience what the will of God is."[5] By putting God's will into practice, we will discover that it lives up to its description (good, pleasing, perfect). Then we will be inclined to give it our approval.

It really works! For a contest, Lisa memorized 1 John 2:17: "The world and its desires pass away, but the man who does the will of God lives forever." She was motivated by a reward—a necklace. As she memorized the verse, God transformed her mind. She realized that the will of God was more important than the necklace. Lisa won the necklace but lost it two weeks later. God gently reminded her what was most important—and Lisa was content with God's will.

TOPIC: *V. Building Character*
SUBTOPIC: *F. Be committed.*
VERSE: *(3) Romans 12:3*
> *By the grace given me I say to every one of you: Do not think of yourself more highly than you ought, but rather think of yourself with sober judgment, in accordance with the measure of faith God has given you.*

CONCEPT

The focus of our first verse in this section (Romans 12:1) was on our surrender and availability to God. The second verse (Romans 12:2) confronted us with the need for growth and change. But talk is cheap. Here in Romans 12:3, commitment means humility and acceptance of God's unique plan and design for us.

COMMUNICATING THE CONCEPT

"Do not think . . . more highly." It's very easy for us to have an exaggerated opinion of ourselves and think that we are the most important people around. Yet everything we are and have is a gift from God, so there is not much room left for boasting.

"Think of yourself with sober judgment." We are to rate our abilities with honesty and realism, not too high and not too low.

"In accordance with the measure of faith . . . given you." This concept is hard to understand. First, let's eliminate what *measure of faith* does not mean. It does not refer to what you have believed, that is, the gospel. Nor does it mean that faith is a quantity that can be divided and given out in portions. It means that each person is given different gifts, functions, and abilities. This is illustrated in the succeeding verses: Romans 12:4-8.

NOTES: 1. Gary Smalley, *The Key to Your Child's Heart* (Waco, Tex.: Word, Inc., 1984), page 139.

2. Betty Skinner, *Daws* (Colorado Springs, Colo.: NavPress, 1974, 1987), page 30.

3. Bill Gothard, "Conscience," *Institute in Basic Youth Conflicts* (1975), page 1.

4. Gothard, "Conscience," page 28.
5. John Murray, *The Epistle to the Romans*, Volume 2 (Grand Rapids: Eerdmans Publishing Company, 1968), page 115.

VI. GREAT BIBLE TRUTHS

"Great Bible Truths" introduces five great Bible truths: Forgiveness, the Word of God, the Second Coming of Jesus Christ, the Church, and the Lord is our Shepherd. Each is presented at the understanding level of an elementary child. The Twenty-third Psalm, perhaps the best-known and best-loved Bible passage, is to be memorized in its entirety. Remember, familiarity doesn't necessarily mean understanding. Carefully discuss the meaning of each verse as your child memorizes it.

Your child did great!!! With the completion of level one of "Great Bible Truths," your child will have memorized 36 key passages of Scripture. If level two has been finished, 72 verses are tucked away in his or her mind. If you are finishing level three, your child has memorized 108 Bible verses. Finishing any of the levels calls for a celebration. Celebrating helps reinforce the importance and significance of this accomplishment.

We hope that you have started your child on a lifetime habit that will continue to develop and enhance his or her walk with God. It is encouraging for children to experience God bringing verses to their minds when they don't have their Bibles open.

REVIEW PLAN

1. As you begin "Great Bible Truths," remember to add "Enjoying God" to your weekly review, along with "Understanding Salvation," "Knowing God," and "Growing as a Christian."
2. Be sure to keep reviewing your "Building Character" verses daily.
3. Learn one verse of "Great Bible Truths" weekly and then add it to your daily review.

TOPIC: *VI. Great Bible Truths*
SUBTOPIC: *A. Forgiveness*
VERSE: *(1) 1 John 1:9*
> *If we confess our sins, he is faithful and just and will forgive us our sins and purify us from all unrighteousness.*

CONCEPT

Because Jesus died for our sins and therefore saves us from the consequences of sin, God promises to forgive us when we confess our sin.

COMMUNICATING THE CONCEPT

"Confess." To confess is to acknowledge sin and guilt and to agree with God that something is not right. It is an outward sign of repentance and faith. Confession should be as specific as possible, as opposed to "forgive me for my sins." This is particularly helpful for a child, for it helps to reinforce what is specifically right and wrong.

"Faithful and just." God will be faithful to keep His promise of forgiveness and will be just in His dealings.

What does it mean to be forgiven? When God forgives, it's as though He has erased all record of that sin. Isaiah 43:25 says, "I am he who blots out your transgressions." He even erases the thought of your sin from His memory! (See Jeremiah 31:34.) It also means that we are expected to forgive others: "Forgive as the Lord forgave you" (Colossians 3:13).

"Unrighteousness." *Righteousness* means to be exactly as God wants us to be. The prefix "un" means "not, lack of, or opposed to." So *unrighteousness* refers to ways we act and think that do not please God. He will forgive us for those things that are "not-right."

Application help. The best way to communicate this concept of forgiveness is to do it! An easy way for children to think of prayer is to think of "thank You prayers," "I'm sorry prayers," and "please prayers." Make a list of items to pray for in each category before you start, and then pray together through your lists.

TOPIC: *VI. Great Bible Truths*
SUBTOPIC: *A. Forgiveness*
VERSE: *(2) Colossians 3:13*
Forgive whatever grievances you may have against one another. Forgive as the Lord forgave you.

CONCEPT

Not only are we to enjoy the forgiveness that we receive from God, but we are also to forgive others in the same way that God forgives us.

COMMUNICATING THE CONCEPT

How do you ask for forgiveness? When you have wronged someone and need to be forgiven, just to say "I'm sorry" is not enough. It leaves the other person without a clear response. Most will simply answer, "That's okay." Whether forgiveness has taken place will be unclear.

A better request is, "I'm sorry. Will you please forgive me?" The answer to this will either be a "yes" or a "no." Whenever a wrong needs to be righted, this is a good formula to follow.

"Grievances." A *grievance* is a complaint that you have about another person because his behavior hurt or angered you (NASB: "complaint").

How has the Lord forgiven you? This stimulating discussion question can help with your review of the last memory verse. See how many items you can add to your prayer lists.

It would be a good idea to review the suggestions under "Building Character" V, B3.

TOPIC: *VI. Great Bible Truths*
SUBTOPIC: *A. Forgiveness*
VERSE: *(3) Matthew 18:21-22*

> *"Lord, how many times shall I forgive my brother when he sins against me? Up to seven times?" Jesus answered, "I tell you, not seven times, but seventy-seven times."*

CONCEPT

There is no limit on how many times we should forgive others.

COMMUNICATING THE CONCEPT

Who's asking? Peter is asking. He thought there ought to be a limit on how often he needed to forgive his brother Andrew and other friends.

"Seventy-seven times." The rabbis had a rule that you should forgive three times and no more! Peter may have thought he was being big-hearted in suggesting seven times. The thrust of Jesus' answer was that we are to forgive more times than anyone would ever think possible. Don't even count! We are to forgive without ever stopping.

Use a tape recorder. Tape recorders are great memory helps. Using a review cassette tape will greatly enhance learning and retention. We found that a particularly effective time to play a review tape for our sons is at bedtime after the lights are out.

TOPIC: *VI. Great Bible Truths*
SUBTOPIC: *B. The Word of God*
VERSE: *(1) 2 Timothy 3:16*
All Scripture is God-breathed and is useful for teaching, rebuking, correcting and training in righteousness.

CONCEPT

We can have confidence in the Bible because all of it is inspired by God.

COMMUNICATING THE CONCEPT

Is it just another book? Many people ask this question about the Bible. The answer is *no*. The Bible was written over a time span of 1600 years, by forty different authors from every walk of life (political leaders, philosophers, fishermen, soldiers, a doctor, a tax collector, a king, etc.). It was written on three continents, and in three languages (Hebrew, Aramaic, and Greek).[1] In spite of all this, it is one book with one unified and continuous theme. How could this happen? Because it is inspired by God.

"God-breathed" (inspired). Let's start with what *inspired* doesn't mean. It doesn't mean that the Scriptures are inspiring, like a great poem (although they are). Neither does it mean that just the ideas behind the Scriptures are inspired. It is the actual written product that is inspired or God-breathed. The Scripture is not only man's word; it is "God's word spoken through man's lips or written with man's pen."[2] The Holy Spirit exerted a supernatural influence on the various writers to produce a product that was exactly as God wanted. Because it is God's Word, and He does not lie, we can have total confidence in the truthfulness and accuracy of the Scriptures.

TOPIC: *VI. Great Bible Truths*
SUBTOPIC: *B. The Word of God*
VERSE: *(2) Mark 13:31*
> *"Heaven and earth will pass away, but my words will never pass away."*

CONCEPT

The Word of God lasts forever.

COMMUNICATING THE CONCEPT

"Heaven and earth will pass away"? This verse says Heaven and earth will definitely pass away. Various Bible teachers differ as to exactly when, but we do know that the timing is related to the Second Coming of Christ. "The day of the Lord will come like a thief. The heavens will disappear with a roar; the elements will be destroyed by fire, and the earth and everything in it will be laid bare [will be burned up]" (2 Peter 3:10).

Will anything last? Yes, God says that there are three things that will last forever: Himself (Psalm 90:2), the souls of men (John 3:16), and the Word of God (Mark 13:31).

We save what's important and valuable. What type of items do we save in scrapbooks or tuck into desk drawers? Which baseball cards do our children save instead of trade? Those they deem important and valuable. That parallels one of the reasons that God will keep and preserve His Word forever. Besides Himself, God will preserve just two things: us and the Bible. That makes the Bible very valuable!

TOPIC: *VI. Great Bible Truths*
SUBTOPIC: *B. The Word of God*
VERSE: *(3) Proverbs 30:5*
Every word of God is flawless.

CONCEPT

So far we've learned that the Bible is God's Word and will last forever. This memory verse adds the concept that God's Word is completely reliable. It is exactly as God intended it to be.

COMMUNICATING THE CONCEPT

"Word of God." Make sure it is clear that the *Word of God* refers to the Bible.

"Flawless." What does it mean for something to be flawless? It means perfect, without error, reliable. How reliable would a road map be that was full of mistakes? Would you use it to help you drive across the country for vacation? It could lead you the wrong way and get you into lots of problems.

God's Word is always correct. It has no mistakes in it. It will never tell you to go the wrong way or do the wrong thing. You will never get in trouble for following what it says.

How much of the Bible is flawless? Emphasize and highlight the first word of the verse: *every*. Check for understanding with this simple question: "If 'every word' is flawless, then how much of the Bible is accurate and reliable?"

173

TOPIC: *VI. Great Bible Truths*
SUBTOPIC: *C. The Second Coming*
VERSE: *(1) Acts 1:11*

> *"This same Jesus, who has been taken from you into heaven, will come back in the same way you have seen him go into heaven."*

CONCEPT

Jesus is coming back.

COMMUNICATING THE CONCEPT

Who says so? Before beginning to memorize this verse, it would be helpful to review the setting. Jesus had been crucified. He had been raised from the dead and is now with His disciples in Jerusalem. Read Acts 1:8 (a future memory verse) together. What did Jesus tell them they were to be? Then what happened? (See verse 9.) While the disciples watched Jesus ascend into Heaven, who came and stood by them? (See verse 10.) What did they say?

"In the same way." This phrase may refer to the cloud. It could also mean that Jesus will come back physically, personally, and visibly (Luke 21:27).

When is He coming? Good question! Memorize the next verse.

TOPIC: *VI. Great Bible Truths*
SUBTOPIC: *C. The Second Coming*
VERSE: *(2) Matthew 24:44*
> *"You also must be ready, because the Son of Man will come at an hour when you do not expect him."*

CONCEPT

We don't know when Jesus will return, so we must work at always being ready to meet Him.

COMMUNICATING THE CONCEPT

"Son of Man." Jesus often referred to Himself as the Son of Man. He did this to help identify Himself as the coming Messiah of the Old Testament. The coming Messiah was described as "one like a son of man" in Daniel 7:13-14. "Son of Man" also helps us to remember that Jesus is not only God. He was also born as a man, tempted as we are, and able to understand our weaknesses. However, because He was also God, He did not sin (Hebrews 4:15).

When is He coming? We don't know. "No one knows about that day or hour, not even the angels in heaven, nor the Son, but only the Father" (Matthew 24:36).

How can we "be ready"? This will make a good discussion question. Peter said that as we wait, we "ought to live holy and godly lives" (2 Peter 3:11). We can be ready by learning what is right through reading the Bible, praying, and asking God to help us do what is right.

Then, when Jesus returns, we won't be ashamed of our behavior (1 John 2:28).

TOPIC: *VI. Great Bible Truths*
SUBTOPIC: *C. The Second Coming*
VERSE: *(3) Colossians 3:4*
When Christ, who is your life, appears, then you also will appear with him in glory.

CONCEPT

So far we have learned that Jesus is coming back and that we must work at being ready for His return. Now we learn of the impact His coming will have on our lives.

COMMUNICATING THE CONCEPT

"When." Even though we don't know the date of the "when," we know its certainty is as sure as if it had already happened.

"Christ, who is your life." Jesus is the source of our new lives, the pattern for our lives, and the Lord of our lives. He is everything to us. Paul expressed the same thought in Philippians 1:21 when he said, "To me, to live is Christ."

"Appear with him in glory." To appear with Christ in glory is to attain His likeness. "We know that when he appears, we shall be like him" (1 John 3:2). Not only will we be transformed to be like Christ, but He will take us to be with Him. "I will come back and take you to be with me that you also may be where I am" (John 14:3).

> Our citizenship is in heaven. And we eagerly await a Savior from there, the Lord Jesus Christ. (Philippians 3:20)

TOPIC: *VI. Great Bible Truths*
SUBTOPIC: *D. The Church*
VERSE: *(1) Ephesians 2:22*
> *In him you too are being built together to become a dwelling in which God lives by his Spirit.*

CONCEPT

This verse begins a section of Scripture on the Church and reminds us that a church is not a building; it's a group of Christians. On Sunday and often at other times, Christians meet together in a building that is called something like First Baptist Church or Grace Community Church. We need to remember that the name refers to the group of people inside the building. Bricks and windows and carpets do not make a church; people do, and special people at that.

177

COMMUNICATING THE CONCEPT

"In him." Be sure that it is clear that this phrase refers to Jesus. To be "in Christ," means to be a Christian, to be "a new creation" (2 Corinthians 5:17). We could begin this verse by saying, "Because you are a Christian."

"Together." This word refers to other Christians.

"A dwelling place in which God lives." God lives and dwells in His people through His Holy Spirit, whom we received when we became Christians. What's the dwelling place in which God lives? A building? No, He lives in us! "The Most High does not live in houses made by men" (Acts 7:48). Who are some of the people that make up your church? Where is your church when no one is in the church building?

TOPIC: *VI. Great Bible Truths*
SUBTOPIC: *D. The Church*
VERSE: *(2) Psalm 122:1*
I rejoiced with those who said to me,
"Let us go to the house of the LORD."

CONCEPT

We should be happy at the opportunity to meet with other Christians and attend church.

COMMUNICATING THE CONCEPT

"House of the LORD." For us as Christians, the house of the Lord, or the Lord's house, is another name for a place where we come together to worship. "My house will be called a house of prayer" (Matthew 21:13).

Sunday morning attitudes. Have you ever complained about going to church because it will make you miss a part of your favorite ball game or keep you from getting a little extra sleep? What should be our attitude about going to church?

TOPIC: *VI. Great Bible Truths*
SUBTOPIC: *D. The Church*
VERSE: *(3) Ephesians 4:16*
From him the whole body, joined and held together by every supporting ligament, grows and builds itself up in love, as each part does its work.

CONCEPT

Being a part of a local church is not like going to a concert or a ball game and being a spectator. God wants everyone involved and working in his or her church. No spectators allowed!

COMMUNICATING THE CONCEPT

"From him." Who does "him" refer to? Ephesians 4:15 identifies "him" as Christ. Notice too that the growth of the Church comes from Christ, who is the Head of the Church (Colossians 1:18).

"The whole body." What does "body" refer to? Colossians 1:18 is a good verse to use in answering that question: "[Jesus] is the head of the body, the church." Be sure that this is well understood, or else Ephesians 4:16 could take on a greatly different meaning!

"Joined and held together by every supporting ligament." Paul compares the Church to a human body, which is held together by individual ligaments and muscles. Can you imagine what it would be like if nothing held our bones together? Just as ligaments and muscles hold our bodies together, what holds the Church together? This verse says that individuals like you and me hold the Body of Christ together.

"As each part does its work." When each of us as individual members of a local church is involved in working at and helping the church, what are the results? It grows and becomes more loving. What are some characteristics of a loving church?

Write a paraphrase. This would be a good verse to write your own paraphrase of, to ensure perfect understanding. Make sure that the concept is clear to the child before he puts the verse into his own words.

Under his direction the whole body is fitted together perfectly, and each part in its own special way helps the other parts, so that the whole body is healthy and growing and full of love. (Ephesians 4:16, TLB)

Understanding tip. Whenever you review these verses on the Church, it would be helpful to check for understanding by asking simple review questions, such as, "What does the 'body' refer to?" or "What does this verse mean?"

TOPIC: *VI. Great Bible Truths*
SUBTOPIC: *E. The Lord is my Shepherd.*
VERSE: *(1) Psalm 23:1*
The Lord is my shepherd, I shall not be in want.

CONCEPT
With this verse your child will begin to memorize not only one of the great chapters of the Bible, but also his or her first entire chapter.

UNDERSTANDING THE PASSAGE
"Shepherd." Why do sheep need a shepherd? Because they don't know how to take care of themselves. They get lost easily and need large amounts of care. In Matthew 9:36, Jesus compares people to sheep. He says they are "helpless, like sheep without a shepherd."

God often refers to us as sheep. A good project would

be to list the ways in which we are similar to sheep. This would also be a good time to review Isaiah 53:6. In what ways is the Lord like a shepherd to us? Read John 10:11-13.

"I shall not be in want." What kind of shepherd would let his sheep go thirsty and hungry? When the Lord is our Shepherd, He takes good care of us because He is the Good Shepherd (John 10:11). His care is the best we could ever want.

TOPIC: *VI. Great Bible Truths*
SUBTOPIC: *E. The Lord is my Shepherd.*
VERSE: *(2) Psalm 23:2*
He makes me lie down in green pastures, he leads me beside quiet waters.

UNDERSTANDING THE PASSAGE

"He makes me lie down in green pastures." Sheep are very timid animals and very easily frightened. W. Phillip Keller says that sheep will only lie down and relax if they are not scared, not bothered by flies and bugs, and have been well fed.[3] A shepherd who has gone to McDonald's for a hamburger would have a hard time protecting and caring for his sheep. They wouldn't be lying down. They'd be hungry, scared, and looking for a fly swatter. Ask your child, "What are some things that scare you? How can knowing that the Lord is a close-by

Shepherd help you overcome these fears?"

"He leads me beside quiet waters." "When sheep are thirsty they become restless and set out in search of water to satisfy their thirst. If not led to good . . . supplies of clean, pure water, they will often end up drinking from the polluted pot holes where they pick up . . . internal parasites . . . and other germs."[4]

God does the same for us. If we follow His leading and instructions, He'll only let us feed on what is good for us and doesn't hurt us. The instructions He gives us are for our good. What are some things that we could take into our minds or bodies that would be bad for us? God wants us to stay healthy, both physically and spiritually.

TOPIC: *VI. Great Bible Truths*
SUBTOPIC: *E. The Lord is my Shepherd.*
VERSE: *(3) Psalm 23:3*
He restores my soul. He guides me in paths of righteousness for his name's sake.

UNDERSTANDING THE PASSAGE

"He restores my soul." W. Phillip Keller tells us that a "cast down" sheep is one that has turned over on its back and is unable to get up again, no matter how hard it tries, without the help of the shepherd.[5] A "cast down" sheep is an easy target for a hungry predator. Is the shepherd mad when he finds a cast down sheep? No, he rejoices that nothing worse has yet happened, and he gently and lovingly sets it back on its feet.

When we fail, make mistakes, get angry and frustrated, feel helpless, does God just leave us alone and wait for us to get back on our feet? No, as our Good Shepherd, He rejoices that nothing worse has yet happened. And He gently and lovingly lifts us up and restores us. "God is . . . an ever-present help in trouble" (Psalm 46:1).

"He guides me." Sheep left on their own not only wander, but they will repeatedly wander to the same places. Soon they will have eaten all the food, polluted the water, and attracted bugs and disease. A sheep left to his own wanderings creates for himself a lot of problems. It's the job of the shepherd to lead the sheep over new paths to fresh fields and clean water.

Isaiah 53:6 says we are just like sheep, always turning to go our own way, doing what we want. As with sheep, our wanderings will get us in trouble. The Lord wants us to follow Him. He leads us in the right places and has us do those things that are good for us.

TOPIC: *VI. Great Bible Truths*
SUBTOPIC: *E. The Lord is my Shepherd.*
VERSE: *(4) Psalm 23:4*
> *Even though I walk through the valley of the shadow of death, I will fear no evil, for you are with me; your rod and your staff, they comfort me.*

UNDERSTANDING THE PASSAGE

"The valley of the shadow of death." During the hot, dry summer season, a shepherd often takes his sheep high into the mountains where the days are cool and the grass is green. Can you imagine wearing a heavy wool coat in the summer? To get to the high pastures, a shepherd will often follow the valleys made by the streams coming down the mountains. Coyotes and wolves and other predators are often hiding along the way. Rock slides and sudden violent storms can make it a frightening and dangerous trip.

It is as though death is hiding in the shadows, yet the sheep are not afraid, because they know the shepherd is there with them to protect them. Whenever we go through dangerous and frightening times, our Shepherd is there with us to protect us.

"Your rod and your staff." A shepherd's rod is a stick that he uses as a club. He uses it to drive off a predator that is attacking his sheep, or he might throw it at a sheep that is wandering into a dangerous situation to send it back to the herd. For us, the Good Shepherd uses His Word to keep us from wandering into trouble or dangerous situations. "How can a young man keep his way pure? By living according to your word" (Psalm 119:9).

A shepherd's staff is a long stick with a hook on one end. The shepherd uses the hook "to reach out and catch individual sheep . . . and draw them close to himself for intimate examination. . . . The staff is also used for guarding the sheep."[6] For us as Christians, God uses the Holy Spirit living in us to draw us close to Him and to help guide us. We have no need to fear in frightening circumstances. The protection and direction of His Word and the presence of His Holy Spirit will comfort us.

TOPIC: *VI. Great Bible Truths*
SUBTOPIC: *E. The Lord is my Shepherd.*
VERSE: *(5) Psalm 23:5*
You prepare a table before me in the presence of my enemies. You anoint my head with oil; my cup overflows.

UNDERSTANDING THE PASSAGE

"**You prepare a table before me.**" W. Phillip Keller tells us that the shepherds would go ahead of the sheep and prepare the new fields for grazing. They would remove poisonous weeds, clean leaves and sticks from where the sheep would drink, and drive away predators.

The sheep were assured of good food because the shepherd went ahead.

So it is for us. Our shepherd has gone ahead of us (Hebrews 4:14), and He knows what's good and also what's harmful for us. Because He loves us, He wants us to have only those things that are good and helpful for us.

"You anoint my head with oil." Have you ever noticed how many flies and other insects there are around a farm or a zoo? During the summer, there is a particular kind of fly that likes to crawl on the face of sheep and lay its eggs inside their noses. This is very painful for the sheep, and as a result sheep are often scared of flies as they buzz around. It was the job of a shepherd to put a fly repellent made with oil on the head of the sheep to keep these flies away.

What are some of the little things that "bug" you? By praying and reading the Scriptures, God can change our attitude and "debug" us! Those little problems flying around just won't bother us. Instead of worrying, He can give us peace. What memory verse has talked about worry and peace? (Philippians 4:7).

Having your devotions is like putting on insect repellent or suntan lotion. You need to do it more than once for it to be effective. We need to allow God to put His "lotion" on us by having our devotions every day.

"My cup overflows." The word *cup* often refers to our life and its content. Here our life is overflowing with good. "I have come that they may have life, and have it to the full" (John 10:10).

TOPIC: *VI. Great Bible Truths*
SUBTOPIC: *E. The Lord is my Shepherd.*
VERSE: *(6) Psalm 23:6*
Surely goodness and love will follow me all the days of my life, and I will dwell in the house of the LORD forever.

UNDERSTANDING THE PASSAGE

"Surely goodness and love." As David thinks back over the loving care of the Good Shepherd, this is his summary: "Surely goodness and love will follow me all the days of my life." This will be our summary also if we allow the Lord to be our Good Shepherd.

"I will dwell in the house of the LORD." "Actually, what is referred to by 'house' is the family or household or flock of the Good Shepherd. The sheep is so deeply satisfied with the flock to which it belongs, with the ownership of this particular shepherd, that it has no wish to change whatever."[7]

"You will fill me with joy in your presence" (Psalm 16:11).

NOTES: 1. Josh McDowell, *Evidence That Demands a Verdict* (San Bernardino, Calif.: Here's Life Publishers, 1972), page 18.
2. J.D. Douglas, ed., *The New Bible Dictionary* (Grand Rapids: Tyndale House Publishers, 1962), page 564.
3. W. Phillip Keller, *A Shepherd Looks at Psalm 23* (Grand Rapids: Zondervan Publishing House, 1970), page 35.
4. Keller, *A Shepherd Looks at Psalm 23*, page 50.
5. Keller, *A Shepherd Looks at Psalm 23*, page 60.
6. Keller, *A Shepherd Looks at Psalm 23*, page 100.
7. Keller, *A Shepherd Looks at Psalm 23*, page 137.

SECTION THREE

SEVEN MINUTES WITH GOD
How to Plan a Daily Quiet Time
by Robert D. Foster

It was in 1882 on the campus of Cambridge University that the world was first given the slogan:

"Remember the morning watch."

Students like Hopper and Thornton found their days "loaded" with studies, lectures, games and bull sessions. Enthusiasm and activity were the order of the day. These dedicated men soon discovered a flaw in their spiritual armor—a small crack which if not soon closed, would bring disaster.

They sought an answer and came up with a scheme they called the morning watch—a plan to spend the first minutes of a new day alone with God, praying and reading the Bible.

The morning watch sealed the crack. It enshrined a truth so often obscured by the pressure of ceaseless activity that it needs daily rediscovery: To know God, it is necessary to spend consistent time with Him.

The idea caught fire. "A remarkable period of religious blessing" followed, and culminated in the departure of the Cambridge Seven, a band of prominent athletes and men of wealth and education, for missionary service. They gave up everything to go out to China for Christ.

But these men found that getting out of bed in time for the morning watch was as difficult as it was vital. Thornton was determined to turn indolence into discipline. He invented an automatic, foolproof cure for laziness. It was a contraption set up by his bed: "The vibration of an alarm clock set fishing tackle in motion, and the sheets, clipped to the line, moved swiftly into the air off the sleeper's body."

Thornton wanted to get up to meet his God!

The intimacy of communion with Christ must be recaptured in the morning quiet time. Call it what you want—the quiet time, personal devotions, the morning watch, or individual worship—these holy minutes at the start of each day explain the inner secret of Christianity. It's the golden thread that ties every great man of God together—from Moses to David Livingstone, the prophet Amos to Billy Graham—rich and poor, businessmen and military personnel. Every man who ever became somebody for God has this at the core of his priorities: time alone with God!

David says in Psalm 57:7, "My heart is fixed, O God, my heart is fixed." A fixed and established heart produces stability in life. Few men in the Christian community have his heart and life. One of the missing links has been a workable plan on how to begin and maintain a morning watch.

I want to suggest that in order to get under way, you start with seven minutes. Perhaps you could call it a daily "Seven-Up." Five minutes may be too short, and ten minutes for some is a little too long at first.

Are you willing to take seven minutes every morning? Not five mornings out of seven, not six days out of seven—but seven days out of seven! Ask God to help you: "Lord, I want to meet You the first thing in the morning for at least seven minutes. Tomorrow when the alarm clock goes off at 6:15 a.m., I have an appointment with You."

Your prayer might be, "Morning by morning, O Lord, You hear my voice; morning by morning I lay my requests before You and wait in expectation" (Psalm 5:3).

How do you spend these seven minutes? After getting out of bed and taking care of your personal needs, you will want to find a quiet place and there with your Bible enjoy the solitude of seven minutes with God.

Invest the first 30 seconds preparing your heart. Thank Him for the good night of sleep and the opportunities of this new day. "Lord, cleanse my heart so You can speak to me through the Scriptures. Open my heart. Fill my heart. Make my mind alert, my soul active, and my heart responsive. Lord, surround me with Your presence during this time. Amen."

Now take four minutes to read the Bible. Your greatest need is to hear some word from God. Allow the Word to strike fire in your heart. Meet the Author!

One of the Gospels is a good place to begin reading. Start with the Book of Mark. Read consecutively—verse after verse, chapter after chapter. Don't race, but avoid stopping to do a Bible study on some word, thought, or theological problem which presents itself. Read for the pure joy of reading and allowing God to speak—perhaps just 20 verses, or maybe a complete chapter. When you have finished Mark, start the Gospel of John. Soon you'll want to go ahead and read the entire New Testament.

After God has spoken through His Book, then speak to Him—in prayer. You now have two and a half minutes left for fellowship with Him in four areas of prayer that you can remember by the word ACTS.

A—*Adoration*. This is the purest kind of prayer because it's all for God—there's nothing in it for you. You don't barge into the presence of royalty. You begin with the proper salutation. So worship Him. Tell the Lord that you love Him. Reflect on His greatness, His power, His majesty, and sovereignty!

C—*Confession* follows. Having seen Him you now want to be sure every sin is cleansed and forsaken. Confession comes from a root word meaning "to agree together with." Apply this to prayer. It means to agree with God. Something happened yesterday you called a slight exaggeration—God calls it a lie! You call it strong language—God calls it swearing. You call it telling the truth about somebody in the church—God calls it gossip. "If I regard iniquity in my heart, the Lord will not hear me" (Psalm 66:18).

T—*Thanksgiving*. Express your gratitude to God.

Think of several specific things to thank Him for: your family, your business, your church and ministry responsibilities—even thank Him for hardships. "In everything give thanks: for this is the will of God in Christ Jesus concerning you" (1 Thessalonians 5:18).

S—*Supplication*. This means to "ask for, earnestly and humbly." This is the part of your prayer life where you make your petitions known to Him. Ask for others, then for yourself. Why not include other people around the world, such as missionaries, students studying abroad, friends in distant places, and above all the people of many lands who have yet to hear about Jesus Christ.

Let's put these seven minutes together:

½	Prayer for guidance (Psalm 143:8)
4	Reading the Bible (Psalm 119:18)
2½	Prayer
	Adoration (1 Chronicles 29:11)
	Confession (1 John 1:9)
	Thanksgiving (Ephesians 5:20)
	Supplication (Matthew 7:7)

7 minutes

This is simply a guide. Very soon you will discover that it is impossible to spend only seven minutes with the Lord. An amazing thing happens—seven minutes become 20, and it's not long before you're spending 30 precious minutes with Him. Do not become devoted to the habit, but to the Savior.

Do it not because other men are doing it—not as a

spiritless duty every morning, nor merely as an end in itself, but because God has granted the priceless privilege of fellowship with Himself. Covenant with Him now to guard, nourish, and maintain your morning watch of seven minutes.

APPENDIX I
Listing of Verses

APPENDIX II
Incorporating *Well-Versed Kids* into the Sunday School

Incorporating *Well-Versed Kids* into your Sunday school program introduces a well-balanced diet of practical Christian living and basic Christian doctrines through the means of Bible memory. Coupled with child-sized applications and fun projects, *Well-Versed Kids* promises to provide exciting, meaningful times around the Word of God for your Sunday school classes.

As with all new programs, prayer, time, and work are essential ingredients. The following list specifically outlines the details of these ingredients for successfully implementing *Well-Versed Kids* into your Sunday school program.

A. CREATING OWNERSHIP OF *WELL-VERSED KIDS* AMONG THE TEACHERS

1. Form a *Well-Versed Kids* committee with one representative from each Sunday school department that will be using the program. It's important for the teachers to feel that *Well-Versed Kids* is *their* program. The responsibilities of the committee include:

a. Praying faithfully for the children in Sunday school and the use of *Well-Versed Kids*.
b. Sponsoring promotional activities.
c. Communicating with all the departments.
d. Knowing the program thoroughly before it begins so that the committee members can answer questions from teachers and parents.
e. Planning and leading a motivational, informative seminar for parents and teachers when the program commences.
f. Deciding the rewards.

2. Have each committee member complete the study on the Bible and Scripture memory (Appendix IV). A group discussion will enhance understanding.

B. PROMOTING *WELL-VERSED KIDS* TO THE CONGREGATION

1. Introduce *Well-Versed Kids* in the church bulletin several Sundays before it actually begins to help generate prayer support. Using simple cartoons along with the announcement will help draw attention to the *Well-Versed Kids* program.

2. Insert a flyer explaining the *Well-Versed Kids* program in your church newsletter.

3. Have a "Poster Sunday" on the theme of Bible memory. Use the Sunday school hour for an art class. Display the results in prominent places around the church.

4. Sponsor a parent-teacher seminar to introduce

Well-Versed Kids one or two weeks before it is introduced to the children. Offering the seminar once during the day and once in the evening will allow more people to attend and also communicate the importance of the seminar. The seminar should include:

a. Teaching on the biblical basis for Scripture memory.
b. A challenge to parents and teachers to be actively involved with their children. Children will be excited about Bible memory if it is important to Mom and Dad and their teachers. If Bible memory is not important enough for adults, the children will quickly assume it isn't important for them either.
c. An overview of the *Well-Versed Kids* program to assure that everyone involved understands it.

C. INTRODUCING *WELL-VERSED KIDS* TO THE CHILDREN

The first step in implementing *Well-Versed Kids* is to gain the support of the entire church. The second step is to create enthusiasm among the teachers and parents. When these two steps have been accomplished, it's time to present the program to the children.

1. Start big! If your church has a puppet ministry, ask them to create a short puppet show on Bible memory and being a "well-versed kid."

2. Make the occasion of handing out the *Well-Versed Kids* boxes a special event.

D. KEEPING ENTHUSIASM HIGH

1. Plan a *Well-Versed Kids* party. Children love parties and this one will be both fun and spiritually rewarding. New or more difficult verses can be easily taught in a fun atmosphere. The topics can be reviewed while having a great time. Appendix III lists several Bible memory games and activities. Some of these can be easily adapted for groups.

2. Create a slide show or video. Children love seeing themselves on film. Show the kids learning their verses and reviewing with each other. Include short testimonies as to how God has used the verses in their lives. Using children and adults who are successfully hiding God's Word in their hearts will also serve to give ideas to other parents and teachers.

3. Keep the congregation informed and praying. Once a quarter, have the children take part in the worship service to share a favorite memory verse. For variety, have the children respond to questions with a memory verse. Possibly have some "well-versed adults" give testimonies about how Bible memory has ministered to them.

4. Have rewards. Why? Because rewards are God's idea. In the book of Deuteronomy, Moses sets up a very elaborate system of blessings or rewards. "If you fully obey the LORD your God and carefully follow all his commands I give you today, the LORD your God will set you high above all the nations on earth. All these blessings will come upon you and accompany you if you obey the LORD your God" (Deuteronomy 28:1-2).

Often you hear that love for God should be enough of a motivation for obedience. God in His wisdom realized that His children needed incentives . . . and so do our children. Internal motivation comes from experience. Until experience occurs, external motivation can provide the necessary means to keep children moving toward the goal.

Select appropriate rewards. As you plan your rewards, don't feel that all of them need to be spiritual in nature. For a young boy, a baseball or a baseball ticket may be more motivating than a Christian book that doesn't interest him. The *Well-Versed Kids* program is providing the spiritual input; the reward is providing the motivation.

You will want to plan for two kinds of rewards. A major reward can be given when an entire level of verses is correctly quoted. Intermediary rewards can be given as each main topic is learned. Announce regularly what the big reward will be. In Deuteronomy 28, Moses was very specific about his rewards. Be sure the rewards are worth working for in the eyes of a child.

Some ideas for major rewards:

- a scholarship to a summer camp;
- tickets or a trip to a major league ball game;
- a day at the mall and out to lunch;
- a quality Christian book appropriate to his or her age level.

Some ideas for intermediary rewards:

- buttons (If your church owns a button maker, create *Well-Versed Kids* buttons, possibly to be given out after the first twelve verses are learned);
- Bible bookmarks;
- candy.

Present the rewards. The Congressional Medal of Honor is a round piece of metal hanging from a ribbon. What makes it an honor to receive is that it's presented by the President of the United States before the joint sessions of Congress. If it were mailed in an envelope, it wouldn't be that special. In the same way, make the presentation of the *Well-Versed Kids* awards a special event. One idea is to have the pastor present these rewards in front of the congregation.

5. Assign different Sunday school classes to prepare *Well-Versed Kids* bulletin boards over the course of the year.

6. *Introduce "Vernon the Verse Man."* Young children especially love Vernon. He is simple to make. Draw a large smiling face on a piece of cardboard. The rest of Vernon's body is paper fan-folded and attached under Vernon's chin. Vernon is best used as a review technique. Vernon starts very short. The fan-folds are folded closed. As a child correctly quotes a verse, one of the fan-folds opens. With each correctly quoted verse, Vernon becomes taller. The challenge is to see how tall Vernon can get.

E. DEVELOPING A HEALTHY REVIEW PROGRAM

1. Consistently listening to the children's verses is very important. Teachers, please be faithful to listen to your students every Sunday.

2. It is essential that you build toward quoting the thirty-six verses. After each main topic is learned, listen to the student quote his first six verses, then twelve verses, then eighteen verses, and so forth. It will save time in Sunday school if you give the responsibility of these intermediate goals to the parents.

3. If the parents or teachers are having a difficult time motivating a child, perhaps another adult can help. Does the child have someone he or she highly respects? Try to recruit that adult to help the unmotivated child.

Friends are an important part of a preadolescent's life. Perhaps peer partners can be assigned to call each other during the week. This is a positive use of peer pressure.

4. Progress charts are an easy way to keep track of verses and review. If these charts are posted in each Sunday school classroom, then the teacher or a substitute can see at a glance where a child is.

APPENDIX III
Fun Ways to Learn and Review Verses

"A wise teacher makes learning a joy" (Proverbs 15:2, TLB).

Terry Hall, a well-known communicator and author, said that *variety*, *visuals*, and *involvement* are the three ingredients necessary to keep students learning. The following are several ideas to add these ingredients to your *Well-Versed Kids* program. These are in addition to the ideas already mentioned in the manual.

A. ACTIVITIES AND GAMES

1. *Stick figure art.* Have the students make stick figure drawings of a verse. The rest of the class interprets the art. For example, Psalm 119:105:

Letting them do this on an overhead projector will be a special treat.

2. *Charades.* If the class is large enough, divide it into

groups of three students each and have them act out a verse . . . no talking allowed. The rest of the class must identify the verse.

3. *Pretend stories.* Younger elementary children love making up stories. Have them make up a story about a verse but not use the verse in the story. Can the rest of the class identify the verse?

4. *Short verses.* With older children, have them condense the verse into eight words or less. In their condensation, they may not use the actual words in the verse. Can the rest of the class identify the verse from this brief paraphrase? Ideas 2 and 3 above are also excellent means of checking to see that the meaning of the verse is understood.

5. *Bible Ping-Pong.* This game is especially popular with young children. Starting with the name of the verse, one person says the name, the second person says the address, the first person then gives the first word of the verse, the second person the second word, and so on through the verse until the end, then the address is repeated again.

6. *Scrambled verses.* Print each word of the verse on a separate index card. In random order, pass out the cards to all the class members. They must work together to put the cards in the proper order.

7. *The present game.* This is an especially good game for Christmas or someone's birthday. Wrap up a small gift in a larger box. As the verse is being quoted, pass the box from one child to the next. The child who ends up with the box tries to quote the entire verse, name and

address included. If he is successful, he gets to have the small surprise in the box.

It is particularly fun for the children to see all the teachers playing this game together. Put enough small prizes in the box for the students of the entire class of the teacher who wins.

8. *Stoplight verses.* When you are in the car with your child, every time you come to a stoplight, he or she must quote a verse.

9. *The penny game.* Give the child three pennies and you keep three. When reviewing a topic, each time he quotes a verse correctly, he gets one of your pennies. If he makes a mistake, you get one of his pennies. The game is over when one person gets all the pennies. If the child wins, it would be a small reward to let him keep the pennies.

B. LEARNING CENTERS

Learning centers are a wonderful way to redeem the time for those children who arrive early at Sunday school. Make each center the size of a student's desk. This limits the number of children at any one center. Each center should feature a different activity or verse.

1. *Jigsaw puzzle.* Write out the current verse on a large piece of tagboard or cardboard. Then cut it apart as in a jigsaw puzzle. The student's goal is to put the puzzle together.

2. *Crossword puzzle.* Make a crossword puzzle featuring one subtopic. The following puzzle is from the subtopic "Be dependable" under "Building Character."

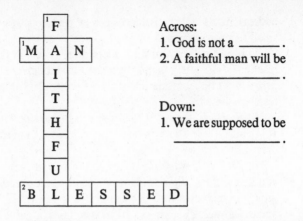

Across:
1. God is not a _____ .
2. A faithful man will be
_____ .

Down:
1. We are supposed to be
_____ .

3. *Blanks.* Write out the current memory verse, leaving blank spaces for all the vowels. The student must fill in the blanks. It will be more difficult if instead you leave blanks for the consonants. Matthew 5:8 would look like this:

M__TTH__W 5:8: BL__SS__D __R__
TH__ P__R__ __N H__ __RT.

__A__ __ __E__ 5:8: __ __E__ __E__ A__E
__ __E __U__E I__ __EA__ __.

4. *Matching.* Write a verse on one index card, the address of the verse on a second index card, and the name of the verse on a third index card. Do this for an entire main topic. The student must make three-way matches.

5. *The listening center.* Have a cassette tape recorder

with headphones for listening to a review cassette tape.

6. *Sandbox verses.* Put several inches of sand in a 9″ x 13″ cake pan. Write each word of a verse on one half of an index card. Glue each one-half index card to a Popsicle stick. The student's job is to stand the "signs" in the sand in the correct order.

APPENDIX IV
Scripture Memory Bible Study

1. a. What do the following verses say about Scripture memory?

   Deuteronomy 6:6-7

   Proverbs 7:1-3

   Colossians 3:16

   b. Is Scripture memory commanded or suggested?

2. In the following verses, summarize the situations and explain how knowing the Scriptures by heart proved to be useful.

Matthew 4:1-11

Acts 13:32-35

3. What are the benefits of Scripture memory?

Psalm 37:31

Psalm 119:11

Proverbs 6:20-23

Isaiah 26:3

Jeremiah 15:16

Luke 6:45

John 15:7

Acts 20:32

Romans 12:2

1 Peter 3:15

4. a. What challenges you the most regarding Scripture
memory?

b. What benefit of Scripture memory is most motivating to you? Why?

c. What does God want you to do regarding Scripture memory?